CHARLES PAHLMAN D. MIN.

Printed for WORLDWIDE DISTRIBUTION by:

PURSUE PUBLICATIONS
INTERNATIONAL, INC.
PO Box 5113   Mentor, Ohio 44060 (USA)
©Copyright 2009, Charles Pahlman, D.Min.
Printed in the United States of America
All Scriptures are from the King James Version Bible.
All italicizing of the Scripture is done by the author.

Third Printing 2011

Dedication and Recognitions

This book is dedicated to a wonderful friend, fellow missionary pastor and trusted mentor of mine, Rev. William Hill ThD.

I would like to especially thank my lovely and supportive wife Denise, who helped me in proofreading this literary work. Tim Pochodzay was most helpful in providing design and editing work, and I could not have been more pleased with his efforts.

I greatly appreciate the two churches that I have pastored (Midway Pentecostal Church, Carlisle, PA and Central Assembly, Mentor, OH), who have been so accommodating and helpful in my missionary efforts over the years.

Lastly, and most of all, I want to praise the Lord of the Harvest, Jesus Christ, for the work of grace in my life and for the passion and opportunities that He has given me for reaching others for Him.

CHARLES PAHLMAN D. MIN.

Table of Contents

CHARLES PAHLMAN D. MIN.

Foreword
by Gene Huff

I was delighted to read and marvel at the material of "The Sprinkle of Nations." It reflects the deep seated burden and involvement of the able author Dr. Charles S. Pahlman. Unlike so many offerings on the subject of World Missions, this book reveals itself as a Premier publication rather than a simple Primer. The "hands on" approach taken by Dr. Pahlman lends itself to the discovery of many, if not nearly all of the approaches in the study of Missions, both foreign and at home.

As you read this book you are awakened in the beginning by the commission placed upon the church by the Lord Jesus Christ. Once the Bible verses and principles have challenged you to the burden of Missions you become possessed with the urgency of the call. When thoroughly committed to the call there can be no delay in praying, giving, and going, wherever and whenever the Holy Spirit leads. Dr. Pahlman demonstrates the commitment personally and is driven by the example of others in years past that have paid the price; made the sacrifice of denial and sometimes even death. The author fully understands that "The blood of the Martyrs is the seed of the church."

This valuable "Sprinkle" reveals the workers, the work, the successes and setbacks of direct missionary involvement. The author introduces to us the heroes from the beginning and brings us into warriors of the present who have gone and are going forth to "conquer" this world for Christ.

It is my sincere hope that this work, "The Sprinkle of Nations" will be a beginning of other kingdom of God writings that will inspire and bring us to our knees praying... "Thy kingdom come, Thy will be done." We will be awaiting further words, Dr. Pahlman.

Sincerely,

Rev. Gene Huff

CHARLES PAHLMAN D. MIN.

Foreword
by Chuck Akers

I remember the urgency I felt in my heart back in 1982 when God first called me to be a missionary. It seemed that there was no way to get on the field in time. So much work needed to be done and there was so little time. Twenty-six years have passed since that day and many things have changed. The urgency to be busy in the labor for souls has only grown. As we know, time is shorter now than it ever was and the world's exploding population clearly is leaving us with more to do now than we ever imagined back then. Everything around us is pointing to the fact that Christ's second coming is upon us. There is no time to be idle in this grand enterprise called Missions. We have come to a specific place in time and the challenge is clear: what we have to do, we must do quickly. Jesus' command is still for His Church to carry the Gospel to the entire world.

I had the privilege of meeting the author Charles Pahlman a number of years ago. It was immediately evident that he was a man with a heart for missions and evangelism. This kind of man is the kind I like to be around. In reality, this is the kind of man God desires to company with!

In his book, The Sprinkle of Nations, Dr. Pahlman makes it clear to anyone willing to submit their reason to Holy Scripture: God's will is for His people to sacrifice whatever may be necessary to carry the Gospel to the lost of our generation. God is intent upon every man, woman and child hearing the message of life-changing truth. Mankind is lost, eternity is long and certain and Jesus is the only answer. So, we know God's desire. We know the basic facts. Now we only need to know what our response to all this will be.

If eighteen years of personal experience on the mission field can teach you anything, surely they have taught me how crucial it is for all of us to maintain a commitment to missions. Likewise, personal experience has proven to me the many dangers faced by the workers. Both of these aspects are well defined in The Sprinkle of Nations. There is no shortage of biblical counsel offered by the author to help us check our commitment and challenge us to more faithful and productive service to our King. I heartily urge you to allow God's Spirit to speak to your heart through the sorely needed message of this book.

Rev. Chuck Akers
- founder of *Beyond Frontiers*

Savior, Sprinkle Many Nations
(Arthur C. Coxe, 1851)

Savior, sprinkle many nations;
Fruitful let Thy sorrows be;
By Thy pains and consolations
Draw the Gentiles unto Thee!

Of Thy cross the wondrous story,
Be it to the nations told;
Let them see Thee in Thy glory
And Thy mercy manifold.

Far and wide, though all unknowing,
Pants for Thee each mortal breast,
Human tears for Thee are flowing,
Human hearts in Thee would rest.

Thirsting as for dews of even,
As the new mown grass for rain
Thee they seek as God of heaven,
Thee as Man for sinners slain.

Savior, lo! the isles are waiting
Stretched the hand and strained the sight,
For Thy Spirit, new creating,
Love's pure flame, and wisdom's light.

Give the word, and of the preacher
Speed the foot and touch the tongue,
Till on earth by every creature
Glory to the Lamb be sung!

CHARLES PAHLMAN D. MIN.

Introduction

Today, the Christian church is living on the brink of the glorious return of Jesus Christ. What a wonderful time to be living for Him! May the hope of His soon return encourage the Saints to be found ever faithful.

When Jesus first commissioned His followers to preach the *Good News* nearly 2000 years ago, the number of souls to be reached with the gospel totaled approximately 250 million. It took 15 centuries for that number to double, but only 350 more years to double again. Today, the growing world is "bulging at the seams" with 6.6 billion people, a number which grows by almost 3 people every second. At this rate, it has been estimated that the world population will double twice during an average 70 year life span!

The major task of the Church is to provide a living message of hope to the dying world, and this mission becomes more challenging as time goes on. Statistics such as those previously stated may come as a shock to us, but the Lord is never taken by surprise. Jesus' *Great Commission,* found at the end of each Gospel as well as the beginning of the book of Acts, has not changed since the time it was first declared. In the same way, Christ's power, wisdom, and grace for His people are still as effective today as then.

In the midst of increasing worldliness and apostasy within the Church world, there are still born again believers dedicating their lives to Biblical standards of holiness and true righteousness. Scripture makes it clear that a life of godliness is a mandate of God for His people (1 Peter 1:16; Hebrews 12:14).

The call to Biblical separation is not, however, the only command from the Lord which the Church must endeavor to obey. Jesus gave this vital charge to His disciples before His ascension: *"Go ye therefore, and teach all nations, baptizing them in the name of the Father, and of the Son, and of the Holy Ghost:"* (Matthew 28:19). Rev. Thomas Peretic, president of Free Gospel Bible Institute has correctly stated: "To have anything less than a world vision is an injustice to the Great Commission."

The same Christ who calls His followers to a life of holiness beckons them to reap the spiritual harvest. A thorough examination of Scripture leaves no doubt that God has called His children to be both holy worshippers and hard workers. There is no excuse for not being both.

Over one hundred years ago, General William Booth, founder of the Salvation Army and one of the greatest preachers of the holiness movement wrote; "'Not called' did you say? 'Not heard the call,' I think you should say. Put your ear down to the Bible, and hear Him bid you go and pull sinners out of the fire of sin. Put your ear down to the burdened, agonized heart of humanity, and listen to its pitiful wail for help. Go stand by the gates of hell, and hear the damned entreat you to go to their father's house and bid their brothers and sisters, and servants and masters not to come there. And then look Christ in the face, Whose mercy you have professed to obey, and tell Him whether you will join heart and soul and body and circumstances in the march to publish His mercy to the world."

The title of this book, The Sprinkle of Nations, is based on the redemptive promise of Isaiah 52:15 - *"So shall He sprinkle many nations..."* The book is written with the understanding that a growing number of Christians are gaining a clearer vision of the church's missionary task and are actively involved in reaching lost souls with their time, talents and treasure. However, I am also aware of the fact that many have yet to *"lift up their eyes, and to look on the fields that are white unto harvest."* I am reminded of a Biblical truth expounded upon by Evangelist Don Rich in one of his sermons, that many churches today have *"...the seed (the gospel) still in the barn!"* (Haggai 2:19) Seeds are meant to be spread and planted, and so must God's Word be in people's minds and hearts in order to take effect.

The purpose of this book is twofold: to fuel the missionary "fire" of those already winning the lost to Christ and discipling believers around the world; and to start a fire in those who are either ignorant of or indifferent to the call of world missions!

As you read this book, I pray that you will repeatedly ask yourself the question posed by the late Malla Moe, "What are we here for, to have a good time with Christians or to save sinners?" By contemplating this thought and allowing it to motivate you to do more to rescue lost souls, you will be following in the footsteps of Christ, the One Who gave His all so that sinners need not perish.

His for the Harvest,

Charles Pahlman D. Min.

CHARLES PAHLMAN D. MIN.

Part One
⍦

The Christ of Missions

For God so loved the world, that He gave His only Son, that whoever believes in Him shall not perish, but have everlasting life. John 3:16

CHARLES PAHLMAN D. MIN.

The prominent 19th century missionary to India and Persia, Henry Martyn, wrote: "The spirit of Christ is the spirit of missions. The nearer we get to Him, the more intensely missionary we become."1 When it comes to Christian missions, it all begins and ends with Christ. A condemned person cannot be saved without Him; and those genuinely redeemed by Christ will have a shared interest in declaring His gospel to others.

Paul the Apostle wrote, *"For the love of Christ constraineth us; because we thus judge, that if one died for all, then were all dead:"* (2 Corinthians 5:14). Adam Clarke, the popular Bible commentator wrote about these words: "We have the love of God shed abroad in our hearts, and this causes us to love God intensely, and to love and labor for the salvation of men."2 How can any say that they love Christ and yet refuse to sincerely care for the unsaved: those made in God's image, who will eternally perish if they do not receive Christ as Savior and Lord?

CHARLES PAHLMAN D. MIN.

Chapter One

~

Christ's Plan and Passion

As committed Christians, we must take seriously our responsibility to share the message of eternal hope with the unsaved. This is not a popular ambition, nor is the task viewed as an easy one. Nonetheless, God has chosen the preaching of His Word and personal evangelism as the primary means of sharing the gospel. As Dwight L. Moody was walking down a Chicago street one day, he saw a man leaning against a lamppost. He gently put his hand on the man's shoulder and asked if he was a Christian. The man angrily raised his fists and exclaimed, "Mind your own business!" "I am sorry if I have offended you," said Moody, "but to be very frank, that is my business!" We are to follow Jesus Christ's example and make reaching lost souls our main business.

Jesus said in Luke 19:10: *"For the Son of man is come to seek and to save that which was lost."* He spoke these striking words nearly 2000 years ago to a man named Zacchaeus, a tax-collector near Jericho. The late British pastor and prolific writer, Charles H. Spurgeon, points out this fact concerning Zacchaeus: "A publican was looked upon as a lost man, who had forfeited his privileges as a son of Abraham; but Jesus restored the lost one, and raised him to a higher position than that which he had occupied by birth."3 This is Christ's specialty: reaching, saving, transforming and elevating the unsaved!

Of course, the conversion of this lost man was not a "spur of the moment" decision on Jesus' part. God the Father, God the Son, and God the Holy Spirit have desired to redeem humanity from eternity past and since man fell into sin. The following verses well demonstrate this:

"In hope of eternal life, which God, that cannot lie, promised before the world began;" (Titus 1:2)

"..., whose names are not written in the book of life of the Lamb slain from the foundation of the world." (Revelation 13:8)

"Forasmuch as ye know that ye were not redeemed with corruptible things, as silver and gold, from your vain conversation received by tradition from your fathers; But with the precious blood of Christ, as of a lamb without blemish and without spot: Who verily was foreordained before the foundation of the world,..." (1 Peter 1:18-20)

This last verse makes the point that God foreknew of man's sin, and knew that he would be in desperate need of a merciful Savior, Who would come as His eternal Son Jesus Christ. Concerning this truth, Albert Barnes wrote, "It was the purpose of God before the worlds were made, to send Him to save lost men...it is not a plan newly formed, or changed with each coming generation, or variable like the plans of men. It has all the importance, dignity, and assurances of stability which necessarily result from a purpose that has been eternal in the mind of God."[4]

In the first chapter of his letter to the Ephesians, Paul expresses the grace, mercy and love He has for these non- Jewish (Gentile) Christian believers. *"According as he hath chosen us in him before the foundation of the world, that we should be holy and without blame before him in love:"* (Ephesians 1:4)

The Apostle wanted them to know that God is no respecter of persons concerning His offer of salvation. One commentator remarks: "The Apostle here shows that God had the Gentiles as much in the thought of His mercy and goodness as He had the Jews; and the blessings of the Gospel, now so freely dispensed to them, were the proof that God had thus chosen them, and that His end in giving them the Gospel was the same which He had in view by giving the law to the Jews,..... that they might be holy and without blame before Him."[5] These comments are in line with Jesus' own words: *"For God so loved the world, that he gave his only begotten Son, that whosoever believeth in him should not perish, but have everlasting life."* (John 3:16)

The German Protestant reformer Martin Luther stated that this familiar verse was the Gospel in miniature! God's love for mankind is brought to clear and effectual focus in the cross of Calvary. It was there that Jesus displayed His great love for a fallen world of sinners.

The Savior's first words from the cross verify this fact when He cried out, *"Father, forgive them; for they know not what they do...."* (Luke 23:34) This loving act of substitution on the cross makes it evident that God does not want anyone to die without His provision of salvation, knowing that the alternative is to go to an everlasting and tormenting hell.

The Apostle Peter recognized that God had this desire for the lost when he wrote *"The Lord is not slack concerning his promise, as some men count slackness; but is longsuffering to us-ward, not willing that any should perish, but that all should come to repentance."* (2 Peter 3:9) This verse demonstrates that if the day of the Lord seems delayed, it is not due to His slackness (Greek.-bradutes: unwilling to execute His promise). It is rather because God is long suffering and is giving time to call the world to repentance.

What Jesus accomplished by dying and shedding His own blood on the cross is aptly illustrated by the following story. "During the last great war an American troopship, the U.S.S. Dorchester, was crossing the North Atlantic when it was torpedoed. The troopship had been crammed -- overfilled, really -- with men needed for the war effort in Europe. As the foundering ship was about to sink it was discovered that there were not life-jackets enough for everyone. Whereupon four military chaplains gave up their life-jackets to four 19-year old soldiers. This act bespeaks much more clearly the provision God's love made for us in the cross."[6] God's plan for the redemption of sinners involved this same kind of sacrificial death of the Savior.

How thankful every born again Christian should be that Christ included them in this eternal plan. Paul was captivated with this thought as he wrote: *"And I thank Christ Jesus our Lord, who hath enabled me, for that he counted me faithful, putting me into the ministry; Who was before a blasphemer, and a persecutor, and injurious: but I obtained mercy, because I did it ignorantly in unbelief. And the grace of our Lord was exceeding abundant with faith and love which is in Christ Jesus. This is a faithful saying, and worthy of all acceptation, that Christ Jesus came into the world to save sinners; of whom I am chief. Howbeit for this cause I obtained mercy, that in me first Jesus Christ might shew forth all longsuffering, for a pattern to them which should hereafter believe on him to life everlasting.."* (1 Timothy 1:12-16)

William M. Tidwell helps to illustrate this kind of gratitude when he writes: "It is said that a man was seen in a cemetery at Nashville, Tennessee, weeping bitterly. When asked the cause he replied, 'I was recruited during the Civil War. I had a large family and a very sick wife. We were very poor and it looked as though my family would all starve. But I had a friend who was not quite old enough to be drafted. He went to the authorities and stated the case and asked to become my substitute. He was accepted. He took my place. He was killed in battle and is buried here. This is his grave. He died for me. That is what makes me weep. I am living because he is dead.'" [7]

This brief tale reminds me of the following quote, "When we think of the substitutionary death of Christ, it seems that that should be sufficient to break our hearts with gratitude." [8]

How marvelous is God's plan to redeem lost man. Those who have experienced Christ's redemptive grace should be motivated and determined to share this good news message with all who have yet to receive it.

1   http://home.snu.edu
2   PowerBible CD
3   The PowerBible CD; Spurgeon Devotional Commentary;
4   PowerBible CD
5   PowerBible CD
6   Victor Shepherd; Sermon: A Note on God's Love
7   http://elbourne.org/sermons/
8   Effective Illustrations

Chapter Two

~

Christ's Provision

A careful examination of the Bible makes evident that the plan of redemption was never man's idea. Since time immemorial, mankind as a whole has had an erroneous concept of salvation. This fact is best illustrated in the Genesis account of Adam and Eve in the Garden of Eden. This incident is actually the initial event in man's flawed attempt to redeem himself. The major portion of the account follows: *"And when the woman saw that the tree was good for food, and that it was pleasant to the eyes, and a tree to be desired to make one wise, she took of the fruit thereof, and did eat, and gave also unto her husband with her; and he did eat. And the eyes of them both were opened, and they knew that they were naked; and they sewed fig leaves together, and made themselves aprons. And they heard the voice of the Lord God walking in the garden in the cool of the day: and Adam and his wife hid themselves from the presence of the Lord God amongst the trees of the garden. And the Lord God called unto Adam, and said unto him, Where art thou? And he said, I heard thy voice in the garden, and I was afraid, because I was naked; and I hid myself."* (Genesis 3:6-10)

Please take careful notice, Adam and Eve had desperately tried to cover their shame with fig leaves but they could not. Only a righteous God could provide such a covering of sin. Later in Scripture we learn that God required a blood sacrifice to atone for sin. Leviticus 17:11 states *"For the life of the flesh is in the blood: and I have given it to you upon the altar to make an atonement for your souls: for it is the blood that maketh an atonement for the soul."*

What God did in the garden for Adam and Eve was a defining sacrifice, the first sign of the coming Lamb of God Who would shed His blood for a world of sinners so that their sin and shame might be covered. John the Baptist would declare some 4000 years later at the baptism of

Jesus, *"...Behold the Lamb of God, which taketh away the sin of the world."* (John 1:29)

A key prophecy regarding the gospel found in the book of Isaiah announces the provision of the atoning work of Christ for a fallen world; it is found in Isaiah 52:15; this is the text that the title of the book is based on: *"So shall he sprinkle many nations...."*

In his commentary, Matthew Henry explains Isaiah's words when he writes: "Many nations shall be the better for him, for he shall sprinkle them, and not the Jews only; the blood of sprinkling shall be applied to their consciences, to purify them. He suffered, and died, and so sprinkled many nations; for in his death there was a fountain opened, (Zechariah 13:1). He shall sprinkle many nations by his heavenly doctrine, which shall drop as the rain and distil as the dew. Moses did so only on one nation (Deuteronomy 32:2), but Christ's on many nations."

In a metaphorical way, the sprinkling is performed today every time the gospel of Jesus Christ is proclaimed. Preaching alone does not save anyone, but when one hears and properly applies the Word of God to their heart, the result is regeneration and salvation. God's desire and passion is that His Word of redemption through Christ, would be declared to every person in every nation.

Because of his fallen nature, man's spirit is dead in trespasses and sins (Ephesians 2:1-3). His sinful nature gives himself a depraved mind which is by itself incapable of understanding important spiritual matters such as salvation. Spiritually speaking, sinful man is traveling on a dangerous pathway which leads to eternal destruction. Unregenerate man is following his own way, not God's way. This perilous philosophy of life is called humanism and was first introduced and initially practiced in the pristine Garden of Eden.

The beliefs of Secular Humanism, whose roots are found in Genesis chapter 3, encourages man to forsake the idea of God and His ways. This worldview teaches that man's origin is in the primordial slime, and that he has evolved in all senses to the intricate creature he is today. Humanism promotes the idea that man started as a mere chaotic combination of gases, and through millions of mutations, his body developed into the complex physical machine seen today.

According to humanistic thinking, man began with no intelligence, evolved to limited intelligence through the ages, and now is witness to the explosion of knowledge which has become his hope of the future. It also teaches that man began with superstitions, which in time became quaint religious beliefs, and he continues to evolve spiritually into a higher understanding, eventually recognizing his own divinity. Humanists believe that man started out in a barbaric "survival of the fittest" mode, but has progressively become more civilized to the point where today we are on the verge of universal peace. The bottom-line of secular humanistic philosophy is that man will be the creator and the provider of his own salvation.

According to one author, "This is the New Age gospel. Man's evolution will continue to the full perfecting of the species, until man has become his own savior."9

Thankfully, God did not leave man to his own devices, but showed mercy upon the world by applying His plan of redemption through Jesus Christ. Man's concept of salvation apart from God and His Word results in ultimate destruction. Paul makes this truth apparent in Romans chapters 1-3 when he argues the point that all of mankind, both Jew and Gentile, is guilty of sin before a holy and righteous God. *"For all have sinned, and come short of the glory of God;"* (3:23)

The religion of self-righteousness, sometimes called the gospel of "good works," is man's feeble answer to his spiritual dilemma. Though this concept may be a good attempt on man's part to reach God, it is sadly inadequate. Isaiah describes the insufficiency of man's religion in the following proverb: *"For the bed is shorter than that a man can stretch himself on it: and the covering narrower than that he can wrap himself in it."* (Isaiah 28:20) Though Isaiah was speaking in the context of Israel's false security in overcoming their physical enemies, his words may also be applied to man's even greater spiritual enemies, which are sin and eternal death. Man can do nothing on his own to overcome the penalty and power of sin.

In Isaiah 64:6, the prophet describes man's failed attempt to please God by his own righteousness: *"But we are all as an unclean thing, and all our righteousnesses are as filthy rags; and we all do fade as a leaf; and our iniquities, like the wind, have taken us away."*

All men need the righteousness of Christ in order to make them acceptable in the sight of the one true and Holy God. The writer of Hebrews declared: *"Having therefore, brethren, boldness to enter into the holiest by the blood of Jesus,"* (Hebrews 10:19). Paul's believed this truth and wrote : *"And be found in him, not having mine own righteousness, which is of the law, but that which is through the faith of Christ, the righteousness which is of God by faith:"* (Philippians 3:9)

Christian Missions is simply a mission to tell the story of God's plan of redemption and restoration through the atoning work of Christ. The shedding of Christ's sinless blood was the act which opened up the way for sinful man's transgressions against God to be remitted. For God to forgive sin solely on the basis of His love, without any sacrifice, would be a distortion of His just nature. Since man cannot pay the penalty for his own sin, God, in order to satisfy His righteousness while maintaining His nature of love and mercy, paid the cost Himself – that is what we call atonement.

The following story which helps to illustrate the idea of Biblical salvation is related in the book titled *Six Hours One Friday*: "A missionary in Brazil discovered a tribe of Indians in a remote part of the jungle. They lived near a large river. The tribe was in need of medical attention. A contagious disease was ravaging the population. People were dying daily. A hospital was not too terribly far away—across the river, but the Indians would not cross it because they believed it was inhabited by evil spirits. To enter the water would mean certain death. The missionary explained how he had crossed the river and was unharmed. They were not impressed. He then took them to the bank and placed his hand in the water. They still would not go in. He walked into the water up to his waist and splashed water on his face. It did not matter. They were still afraid to enter the river. Finally, he dove into the river, swam beneath the surface until he emerged on the other side. He punched a triumphant fist into the air. He had entered the water and escaped. It was then that the Indians broke out into a cheer and followed him across. That is exactly what Jesus did!

He told the people of His day that they need not fear the river of death, but they would not believe Him. He touched a dead boy and called him back to life. They still did not believe. He whispered life into the body of a dead girl and got the same result. He let a dead man spend four days in a tomb and then called him out and the people still did not believe Him. Finally, He entered the river of death and after three days and nights He came out on the other side."10

The incarnation of Christ, His impeccable earthly life, His death, burial, resurrection and ascension were all needed to provide salvation for this world of sinners. However, only those who actually hear of Christ's provision of salvation and receive Him and His work for themselves will benefit. The Apostle John writes in John 1:12, *"But as many as received him, to them gave he power to become the sons of God, even to them that believe on his name:"* and in John 3:36, *"He that believeth on the Son hath everlasting life: and he that believeth not the Son shall not see life; but the wrath of God abideth on him."*

Charles G. Finney, the renowned revivalist, said in one of his recorded sermons, "Since this atonement has been made, all men in the race have a right to it. It is open to every one who will embrace it. Though Jesus still remains the Father's Son, yet by gracious right he belongs in an important sense to the race--to every one, so that every sinner has an interest in His blood if he will only come humbly forward and claim it. God sent His Son to be the Savior of the world--of whomsoever would believe and accept this great salvation."11

Concerning the availability of salvation for all sinners, Finney remarks "The doors (of salvation) are always open. Like the doors of Broadway Tabernacle in New York, made to swing open and fasten themselves open, so that they could not swing back and shut down upon the crowds of people thronging to pass through. When they were to be made, I went myself to the workmen and told them by all means to fix them so that they must swing open and fasten themselves in that position. So the door of salvation is open always--fastened open, and no man can shut it--not the Pope, nor the devil, nor any angel from heaven or from hell. There it stands, all swung back and the passage wide open for every sinner of our race to enter if he will."12

The simple message of salvation is that the world's need of a Savior has been provided. What is so desperately needed now is for voices who will proclaim this marvelous offer of salvation to those who are ready to perish. Oswald Chambers was undoubtedly contemplating this same thought when he said, "God is not saving the world; it is done. Our business is to get men and women to realize it."13 This statement holds true for the church throughout all ages. May our merciful God help us to be more like our Savior who made it His primary business to *seek and to save that which is lost."* (Luke 19:10)

9 Phil Morgan sermon on Genesis 3.
10 Max Lucado
11 Charles G. Finney; God's Love for a Sinning World
12 Finney
13 www.forallnations.com

Part Two
⊬

The Call to Missions

CHARLES PAHLMAN D. MIN.

Introduction:

A studious fundamental minister has rightly observed that neither the word "missions" nor "missionary" is found in the Bible.14 Though these terms are used frequently among modern evangelical Christians, they are actually derived from words in the Greek language, the language in which the New Testament was written. The Greek word "apostolos" is translated "apostle," which means, "one sent out with a message." This person has a mission for Christ: another has sent him out, and he bears the message of the sender.

Reliable statistics establish the shameful fact that many Christians in America tend to be generally unaware or just closed-minded concerning the matter of World Missions. In 2005, The Barna Research Group reported the following; "When a nationally representative sample of 614 Senior Pastors was asked to identify the top three ministry priorities for their church in the coming year, not a single ministry emphasis was listed by even half of the church leaders." Barna also reported the following: "The second level of priorities included congregational care efforts, such as visitation and counseling (24%); worship (19%); ministry to teenagers and young adults (17%); missions (15%)-[emphasis mine]; community service (15%); ministry to children (13%); and church fellowship(11%)." 15

When the word missions or missionary is mentioned in today's typical church, many individuals envision some overzealous minister and his family living in a remote part of a hot and humid, insect and snake infested jungle somewhere trying to convert the pagans who reside there. Or perhaps they think of some eccentric introverted Christian who has no other talents and abilities to be exercised here at "home" so the only place for them is on the foreign mission field. However, the Bible does not support these views in any way.

Though Christian missions may involve going to the remote parts of the world, including secluded jungles, it is certainly not limited to that, and neither is missions the work of boring, lonely, and ungifted individuals in the church. World Missions is the mission of Christ for the whole church to reach the whole world!

One of the greatest and most influential men of God in recent centuries was the Moravian minister Count Zinzendorf, who shared his heart's chief desire when he stated, "I have but one passion - it is He, it is He alone. The world is the field and the field is the world; and henceforth that country shall be my home where I can be most used in winning souls for Christ." 16 This exceptional church leader equated loving and seeking after Christ with being wholly given to World Missions.

Missions work involves a wide array of evangelistic duties. When answering the question "What is missions?" one minister answered correctly, "It is all of our work, empowered by the Holy Spirit to proclaim Jesus Christ and share the blessings of the Christian faith with all who are strangers to His grace."17   So then, we can talk about missions whether we are in Pittsburgh or Paris, Miami or Manila, Lima, Ohio or Lima, Peru; missions involves getting the gospel to all people everywhere.

Chapter Three

~

The Undeniable Call

Many are familiar with the adage, "People only hear what they want to hear." It is possible to physically hear the words of another while at the same time mentally and spiritually "tuning out" the content of the message. Such was the case in Isaiah chapter 6 when God told the prophet to preach a message to the people, and also told him what the people's response would be to his words.

God told Isaiah *"...Go, and tell this people, Hear ye indeed, but understand not; and see ye indeed, but perceive not. Make the heart of this people fat, and make their ears heavy, and shut their eyes; lest they see with their eyes, and hear with their ears, and understand with their heart, and convert, and be healed."* (Isaiah 6:9-10) The people refused to hearken to Isaiah's message of salvation and reconciliation to God, and remained willfully deaf to the call that God was directly sending to them through His messenger. Matthew Henry said "Many hear the sound of God's word, but do not feel the power of it."[18]

Sadly, a growing number in the church world today tend to ignore the Biblical message of World Missions in the same way that the people of Isaiah's day ignored his message from God. The message does not necessarily go unheard, but often goes unheeded. Serious Bible readers must agree that the call to World Missions as seen in Scripture is undeniably directed to every believer. The issue of who should actually leave their homes and become foreign missionaries will be addressed later, but it is sufficient to say for now that all Christians should be extremely interested and deeply involved in the task of reaching the lost world for Christ.

Far too many have become either deceived about or distracted from the matter of World Missions. The chief goal of a growing number of local congregations, especially in the Western world, is to fill their own church pews instead of working to spread the Good News throughout the whole world. This idea is largely driven by a wrong view of ministerial success. Mike Stachura said it best when he stated: "The mark of a great church is not its seating capacity, but its sending capacity."19

As a pastor of over eighteen years, I fully realize the need to "begin at home" with the call and mission of winning souls to Christ. The paradigm for missions is well explained in Acts 1:8 where Jesus said *"But ye shall receive power, after that the Holy Ghost is come upon you: and ye shall be witnesses unto me both in Jerusalem, and in all Judaea, and in Samaria, and unto the uttermost part of the earth."*

We desperately need to preach the gospel at home and attempt to win our neighbors to Christ. However, Jesus did not end His mandate for missions in "Jerusalem." Our mission to reach others for Christ must not stop until Christ's cause is taken to the *"...uttermost parts of the earth."* By close observation, one can clearly figure out that undue emphasis placed upon numerical growth tends to encourage the measurement of success by the number of people gathered into a church building. However, it does not appear that God measures success by large numbers alone. Cults and false religions are growing rapidly in these last days, but remain far from the truth of God's plan of salvation.

Church is more than a place for seeking and worshipping God, but is also a place of serving and working for God. One contemporary Christian writer explains this truth further: "Missions is not the ultimate goal of the church. Worship is. Missions exists because worship does not."20 One must be careful not to misunderstand this statement. Lost humanity does not know the true living God and the Savior Jesus Christ, and therefore cannot worship Him. The purpose of missions is to bring the truth of the Savior to the unsaved so that those who receive Him can worship and serve Him just as other born again believers do.

The late J. Pressley Barrett appropriately wrote: "The gospel has been given for the enlightenment of the heathen world, that they might come to Christ and have part in this great salvation. He has made provision for its dissemination, by committing the work of giving it to all nations by the church."21 The mandate that Jesus gave to the Church has never been revoked: it is still pertinent today. One missionary observed, "Had the Apostles stayed in Jerusalem till they had converted their countrymen, Christianity would have been strangled at birth."22

The souls that make it to heaven will be there for three reasons: (1) Jesus paid the price for their redemption on Calvary's cross; (2) someone obeyed Christ's call to tell them about His amazing offer of salvation, (3) they accepted Christ's atoning work for themselves. Knowing these truths, Paul was compelled to write: *"For whosoever shall call upon the name of the Lord shall be saved. How then shall they call on him in whom they have not believed? and how shall they believe in him of whom they have not heard? and how shall they hear without a preacher? And how shall they preach, except they be sent? as it is written, How beautiful are the feet of them that preach the gospel of peace, and bring glad tidings of good things!"* (Romans 10:13-15)

Strictly speaking, Romans 10 is Paul's explanation of Christ's call to the early Church and her Apostles and Evangelists to reach the Gentile world with the gospel. However, in a broader sense, this is Christ's call to the Church of every age. In this passage, Paul details the basic methods whereby the Good News of salvation is to be spread to the lost.

In both Old and New Testaments, the Bible teaches that God's call to World Missions is both individualistic and corporate. Not only does God call individuals to go to specific places and to certain peoples with His message of hope (i.e: Jonah; Paul), but He also calls God's people corporately to be involved in spreading this message to all (i.e. Matthew 28:18-20; Acts 1:8).

The work of Christian Missions is a team effort. In any team, some of the players are more visible and prominent than others. However, the prominent players are well aware of the fact that they could not win the game without the help of the other team members. In the same way, the workers in the true Church must cooperate with one another if the Church is to do the much needed work of

Christian missions in these last days. It has been said, and sadly to our shame, "We Westerners tend to be too individualistic and fail to appreciate how God wants to work through the body of Christ."23 It is only reasonable to conclude that all successful missions work has involved and will continue to involve the work of fellow believers.

The following account helps to relate the previous truth: "William Carey was an English Baptist preacher who had a burden for the people of India. He met with what would become the Baptist Missionary Society, and voiced his concern for the Indian people. After much discussion, Carey said: I will go, but you must hold the ropes! A member of the society replied, And, Mr. Carey, what are the ropes? William Carey replied, Sir, there are two: the first is prayer, and the second is finances. Carey later sailed to India in 1793, and became the Father of Modern-day Missions."24

The "rope holders" are just as important to the work as the ones who descend into the work on the foreign fields; and God rewards them equally. This principle is made evident in this Old Testament text: *"For who will hearken unto you in this matter? but as his part is that goeth down to the battle, so shall his part be that tarrieth by the stuff: they shall part alike."* 1 Samuel 30:24. Here David had resolved that those who stayed at home to care faithfully for the possessions of those who went to war were to have an equivalent share in the rewards of battle. So then, the believers who faithfully support worthy missionaries will share in the heavenly rewards and the approval of the Lord of the harvest. Jesus said in Matthew 10:41: *"He that receiveth a prophet in the name of a prophet shall receive a prophet's reward; and he that receiveth a righteous man in the name of a righteous man shall receive a righteous man's reward."* The World Missions application here is that Christians who stay at home, yet continue to aid those who go into the harvest fields will not go unrewarded by God.

The corporate call to missions is also superbly illustrated in the account given in Acts chapter 13. The Holy Ghost directed the leadership of the Antioch church to set apart Paul and Barnabas, two of the most gifted men in the Kingdom of God, for missionary work. It must be noted that these men were already doing missionary work on their own, but they began at this point to cooperate with the church leaders there who were also missions-minded. Great spiritual and eternal results were accomplished for Christ through them among the heathen because of their cooperative effort.

To adequately discuss the call to missions, it is necessary to contemplate Jesus' words in Mark 16:15, otherwise known as Mark's version of The Great Commission. *"And he said unto them, Go ye into all the world, and preach the gospel to every creature."* These closing words of Jesus to His disciples beg a few questions:

1) <u>Who is being commanded?</u> Notice, Jesus says "Go ye." Though only a few of His disciples were present at the time, I, along with many others, believe that Jesus is speaking to His Church as a whole throughout every age when He gives this mandate for missions. It is only logical to conclude that telling the Good News of the gospel to every creature will necessitate the help of more than the handful of disciples present at the time of Jesus' charge. Hudson Taylor, the legendary missionary to the Chinese, was aware of this when he wrote: "The Great Commission is not an option to be considered; it is a command to be obeyed." 25

2) <u>Where are we to go?</u> Jesus ended His command to go with the words, *"...into all the world."* All humans have the dreadful spiritual disease of sin, and, without help, will endure its eternal penalty of death and hell. Keith Wright states: "Lost people matter to God, and so they must matter to us."

Wherever they may reside, every lost person needs a Christian to bring Christ's message to them. Fulfilling the Great Commission may involve hardship, but every sacrifice made is worth seeing lost souls snatched from the clutches of Satan and sin, and brought nigh unto a loving Savior! The heroic African missionary David Livingstone, who paid a great price to tell the gospel story to the heathen, once said "If a commission by an earthly king is considered an honor, how can a commission by a Heavenly King be considered a sacrifice?" C.T. Studd, another missionary wrote, "If Jesus Christ be God and died for me, then no sacrifice can be too great for me to make for Him." The love of Christ should constrain Christians to be involved in reaching the lost everywhere!

3) <u>When should Christians go?</u> Jesus does not give a starting date or time limit for declaring the gospel during His charge in Mark 16:15. He had already instructed His disciples that the time for them to reach souls with the gospel was present. In John 4: 35, Jesus said, *"Say not ye, There are yet four months, and then cometh harvest? behold,... Lift up your eyes, and look on the fields; for they are white already to harvest."*

One writer observed: "Harvest began about the middle of April in Palestine. The time when the Savior spoke would then be about the middle of December. But the harvest of souls was ripe already."26 Men are dying today: for many, tomorrow will be too late.

4) <u>What is the purpose of our going?</u> Jesus gave instructions about who is to go and where we should go, and He now addresses what Christians are to do when they go: *"...Preach the Gospel."*

A simple band-aid would be of little use as a cure for a life threatening disease. Because mankind's primary problem is sin, nothing but the gospel of Christ can help him escape the consequences of sin's penalty. Paul wrote, *"For the preaching of the cross is to them that perish foolishness; but unto us which are saved it is the power of God....For after that in the wisdom of God the world by wisdom knew not God, it pleased God by the foolishness of preaching to save them that believe."* (1Corinthians 1:18, 21)

Though scores of causes are worthy, the Church's main objective is not to feed the hungry, build hospitals and fight wars. The primary task facing the Church is to declare the message of salvation through Christ. A.B. Simpson summarizes what the gospel does for the lost: "It tells rebellious men that God is reconciled, that justice is satisfied, that sin has been atoned for, that the judgment of the guilty may be revoked, the condemnation of the sinner cancelled, the curse of the Law blotted out, the gates of hell closed, the portals of heaven opened wide, the power of sin subdued, the guilty conscience healed, the broken heart comforted, the sorrow and misery of the Fall undone." 27

It is our privilege as well as our responsibility as Christians to offer to a dying world the spiritual medicine they so desperately need, and we must do so while there is time.

5) <u>Who must we give the gospel to?</u> In His commission to the Church, Jesus answers this important question: *"...to every creature."*

Jesus calls for the evangelizing of all nations. This is a monumental task, but if the Lord commands it, it must be attainable. As of the year 2009, the number of people in the world was estimated to be at least 6.6 billion. To prove the greatness of the task of reaching every creature of this generation, Jay Rodgers, international Director of a world missions ministry named *The Forerunner,* cites the following:

"In biblical terminology, a nation or ETHNOS, is not a geopolitical boundary, but a "peoples group" defined by a common genealogy, history, culture and language. The U.S. Center for World Missions has numbered at least 24,000 distinct ethnic groups which can be viewed in biblical terms as the ETHNE, "the nations," or "peoples groups," that must be reached with the gospel in order to fulfill the Great Commission of Jesus Christ: ...Of these 24,000 peoples groups, there are about 10,000 which have an indigenous witness in the form of a New Testament Church made up of people from their own culture. This leaves 14,000 peoples groups which still must be reached with the gospel in order for the Great Commission to be fulfilled."[28]

We should and must realize that every soul is precious to our gracious God. The Bible verse John 3:16 must convince us that Jesus died for every sinner and compel us to tell every soul that Jesus wants to save them from eternal damnation. The distinguished Christian writer John Stott reiterates the need to preach the gospel to every creature: "We must be global Christians with a global vision because our God is a global God." [29]

The Great Commission ought to be taken seriously by every Christian. For many, however, it has become as some have termed it, The Great Omission! One possible reason for the Great Commission going largely unfulfilled is because of a lack of understanding in many Christians. For some, Church leaders may have failed to properly define for them this vital biblical mandate given by Christ.

One Christian leader gave this clear definition of the Church's task: "Evangelical churches view the Great Commission as a command to preach the gospel of Jesus Christ to every person on the face of the earth, so their missionary efforts center on making Christian converts, assimilating them into viable churches, and training national and international workers for even more effective evangelization in the future."[30]

The call to the duty of reaching the lost for Christ is undeniable. We must not ignore this call, but rise to the challenge in order to please Christ, who would have all men to be saved. (1 Timothy 2:4). Jesus' call to this vital task of reaching the heathen with the gospel was so strong in the African missionary C.T. Studd's mind that he wrote: "Some wish to live within the sound of a chapel bell, I want to run a rescue shop within a yard of Hell." If a larger number of saints shared C.T. Studd's mindset and heart-felt desire, the task of evangelizing the world would undoubtedly be accomplished much more quickly.

14 Kevin Higgins, "Missions, The Great Mandate"
15 www.Barna.org
16 www.evangelismcoach.org
17 Kevin Higgins, "Missions, The Great Mandate"
18 Matthew Henry commentary
19 The Bible Channel, Quotes
20 www.acts29network.org : John Piper quote
21 J. Pressley Barrett; Fruit Bearing Truths and a Bridal Tour of the Mission Field: 1904; pp.17-18.
22 Ibid; p. 59.
23 C. G. Olson; What in the World is God Doing?; p. 85.
24 Dr. W. Jim Britt; (Newsletter, May 2006)
25. Biblical School of World Evangelism publication.
26 People's N.T. Commentary
27 M. Cocoris, Evangelism, A Biblical Approach, Moody; p. 29.
28 The Forerunner.com
29 John Stott; www.TheBibleChannel.com
30 David A. Womack; Spread the Flame; Gospel Publishing House; Springfield, MO; p. 19

Chapter Four

~

The Urgent Call

While healing a blind man, Jesus spoke these compelling words: *"I must work the works of him that sent me, while it is day: the night cometh, when no man can work."* John 9:4. Though Christ was referring to His limited time here on earth, the short time allotted Him to work miracles in the lives of those desperately needing His touch, His words hold an important implication for all Christians.

In his relatively brief epistle, James wrote: *"Be patient therefore, brethren, unto the coming of the Lord. Behold, the husbandman waiteth for the precious fruit of the earth, and hath long patience for it, until he receive the early and latter rain. Be ye also patient; stablish your hearts: The coming of the Lord draweth nigh."* (5:7-8) In this passage, James comforts the first century saints by reminding them that the Lord would deliver them from their trials and persecutions in His pre-ordained time. This text may and should also be used to encourage Christians of every age to remain busy in the work of the Lord, winning souls for Christ.

We should always keep in mind that Jesus is coming back to judge the world in righteousness, but He is also coming back for a harvest of souls. The Lord compared souls to a spiritual harvest on several occasions (John 4:35 and Matthew 9:37-38). Because no one knows the hour of Christ's return, the gleaning of this harvest is extremely urgent. There are two basic steps involved in the call for laborers to harvest souls for the Lord: The Urgent Call for Attention, and The Urgent Call for Action.

The Urgent Call for Attention

It has been mentioned already that Jesus came into this world for one primary reason: *"...to seek and to save lost men."* This fact is unmistakably illustrated by the following account given by Matthew: *"And Jesus went about all the cities and villages, teaching in their synagogues, and preaching the gospel of the kingdom, and healing every sickness and every disease among the people. But when he saw the multitudes, he was moved with compassion on them, because they fainted, and were scattered abroad, as sheep having no shepherd. Then saith he unto his disciples, The harvest truly is plenteous, but the labourers are few; Pray ye therefore the Lord of the harvest, that he will send forth labourers into his harvest."* (Matthew 9:35-38) In this passage, Christ proves that He is no respecter of persons and He will minister to the poorest and lowliest of people. He does not wait for people to come to Him, but takes the initiative to go to where they are.

I believe that there is significance in the fact that Matthew includes this statement about Christ: *"He saw the multitudes."* Even a minimal observation of people will support the idea that most individuals "hear what they want to hear and see what they want to see." Jesus could have chosen to ignore this large, lost crowd.

He could have blamed them for creating their own distressing condition, or sadder yet, could have judged and cursed them. However, our Lord did none of those things. Matthew tells us that He had compassion upon them. Matthew highlights this display of compassion in Jesus because it was such a rare happening in the Jewish world of his day.

Jesus saw what His eye was looking for: those who had need of Him! C. Gordon Olsen says: "The need constitutes the call."31 Jesus was called to these people because they had a need. The sick need the Physician. Jesus paid attention to the cry of the multitude. The Old Testament records that this is exactly what God did for Israel in the days of their bondage in Egypt. *"And it came to pass in process of time, that the king of Egypt died: and the children of Israel sighed by reason of the bondage, and they cried, and their cry came up unto God by reason of the bondage. And God heard their groaning, and God remembered his covenant with Abraham, with Isaac, and with Jacob."* (Exodus 2:23-24)

Jesus used this occasion not only to minister to these souls who He likens to wandering sheep who were

THE SPRINKLE OF NATIONS

lost, lacking, and leaderless, but also uses it to teach a valuable lesson to His disciples. Jesus wanted them to see what He Himself saw. Man is selfish by nature, and so prone to overlook the needs of others. As long as their own needs are met, many people are satisfied. This is a great problem even among professing Christians. Someone wisely observed: "Men are not against you; they are merely for themselves."

To further prove the problem of selfishness in our world, I cite the words of Christian writer Gene Taylor: "Those who comprise our society seem to be consumed with self. The 'me' generation we heard so much of has aged to become the most influential segment of society. So many of the products and services which are popular today are those which are aimed at improving the individual. The 'self-help' books and seminars intended to improve self-image have been embraced by nearly everyone."[32]

Religious people without the mind of Christ have shown themselves to be some of the most self-centered and self –seeking. Think for a moment of the story which has been labeled "The Good Samaritan." Luke records this account for us: *"... A certain man went down from Jerusalem to Jericho, and fell among thieves, which stripped him of his raiment, and wounded him, and departed, leaving him half dead. And by chance there came down a certain priest that way: and when he saw him, he passed by on the other side. And likewise a Levite, when he was at the place, came and looked on him, and passed by on the other side. But a certain Samaritan, as he journeyed, came where he was: and when he saw him, he had compassion on him, And went to him, and bound up his wounds, pouring in oil and wine, and set him on his own beast, and brought him to an inn, and took care of him. And on the morrow when he departed, he took out two pence, and gave them to the host, and said unto him, Take care of him; and whatsoever thou spendest more, when I come again, I will repay thee. Which now of these three, thinkest thou, was neighbour unto him that fell among the thieves? And he said, He that shewed mercy on him. Then said Jesus unto him, Go, and do thou likewise."* (Luke 10:30-37)

The religious men in the story simply ignored the man who was in great need. The priest, whose office should imply not only the duty of kindness but the responsibility of being an example, ignored the helpless plight of his own countryman. These men had ample opportunity to help, but did not for purely selfish reasons. They displayed this behavior even though their own law commanded them to show mercy and help their neighbor (Deuteronomy 22:1-4). What a rebuke to all professors of Christianity who go through life looking only after themselves, never being mindful of those in dire need of the gospel. This was the same charge brought against the rich man who fared sumptuously daily while the poor beggar Lazarus lay at his gate, receiving pity only from the dogs that licked his sores.

God's Word teaches clearly that Christians must take heed to the call to reach others with the gospel. We are stewards of our Master, Jesus Christ. The Scriptures warn that we must all give an account to our Lord, for He has "hired" us as His laborers to work in His fields. Woe to any who willfully ignore the needs of lost souls around them.

It is a fact that the mind must be fully engaged in order for the body to do any work proficiently. Jesus stated in John 4: 35, *"Look on the fields,"* because most humans are so prone to look elsewhere. Even ministers of the gospel can be so taken up with their own local field of labor that they forget or simply ignore the vast multitudes in other parts of the world that need attention and help as well.

Please consider for a moment what Paul wrote to the Philippians: *"For I have no man likeminded, who will naturally care for your state. For all seek their own, not the things which are... Christ's."* (Philippians 2:20-21) One commentator explains Paul's words by writing: "Paul's workers were too closely interested each in his own particular field to give intimate attention to the spiritual condition of the Philippians."[33] To a large degree, this applies as well to today's church world. Concerning spiritual matters, the local established churches get the majority of our attention, while many people elsewhere in the world are completely ignored. Obviously, a single Christian cannot aid and assist every missionary endeavor in every area of the world. However, if the truth be told, too many are doing nothing or very little in the way of reaching those most desperately in need of hearing the true gospel. Remember, there are many people groups of our world who have yet to even hear the name Jesus, let alone have the gospel explained to them. As followers of Jesus, all Christians must pay more attention to His harvest.

Maltbie D. Babcock, the well recognized Presbyterian preacher of the late 19th century, once stated to the Christians of his day regarding the support of foreign missions: "Your wings of love are broken if they cannot fly you across the sea." In order to love, be burdened for, and pray for the lost, especially those who have the least amount of gospel light among them, one must consistently keep in mind their distressing spiritual condition. Each of us must ask ourselves, "Am I paying attention to the harvest today?"

The Urgent Call for Action

Just as Jesus had but a brief time to labor for His Father's kingdom, so it is with believers of every age. Recall Jesus' statement in John 9:4 *"The night cometh when no man can work..."* William Burkitt comments on Christ's striking words by writing: "Here our Savior tells his disciples, that He was sent by God into the world, and had a great work assigned to Him by God, during His abode in it; namely to instruct, reform, and save mankind; and what our Savior says of Himself, is applicable to every one of us in a lower sense; we are sent into the world to work out our own salvation in the first place, and then to promote the salvation of others as much as in us lies."34

Someone has well stated this simple fact: "This generation must reach this generation." We cannot go back to past centuries and preach the gospel: those time periods are gone, and the souls living during those moments in history have now reached their permanent home, heaven or hell, depending on their standing with God. Those who died without Christ are now in hell, not because God did not love them or try to save them, but simply because they did not believe on Jesus Christ to save them from God's wrath upon their sin. (John 3:36)

An accurate definition for hell suggested by one preacher is: "Truth revealed too late!" When souls perish without the Savior, there is no longer any redemptive help available for them. Hebrews 9:27 proclaims, *"And as it is appointed unto men once to die, but after this the judgment:"* According to John Wesley, this verse teaches: "...(that) At the moment of death every man's final state is determined."35 If they would be saved, men must call upon Jesus *"while He is near."* (Isaiah 55:6).

The prolific Christian writer, Carl F. H. Henry affirmed that: "The gospel is only good news if it gets there in time." How true! This is well illustrated by the following story: "Hudson Taylor at Ning-po in China led to Christ a young Buddhist leader, a dealer in cotton. After hearing a message on John 3:14-15, he arose, saying, 'I have long sought the truth, as did my father before me, but without finding it. I have traveled far and near, but have never searched it out. In Confucianism, Buddhism, Taoism, I have found no rest; but I do find rest in what we have heard tonight. Henceforward I am a believer in Jesus.' And he went on to become a leader in spiritual things in the city. Later, upon talking with Taylor, he raised a question not easily forgotten, 'How long have you had the Glad Tidings in England?' Taylor, ashamed, said vaguely that it was several hundreds of years. 'What', exclaimed Nyi in astonishment, 'several hundreds of years! Is it possible that you have known about Jesus so long, and only now have come to tell us? My father sought the truth for more than twenty years,' he continued sadly, 'and died without finding it. Oh, why did you not come sooner?'"36 May we never forget the fact that souls of this hour must be reached by soul-winners of this hour.

Thankfully, many have given their all for the cause of evangelizing the lost for Christ. The church should daily give thanks for individuals willing to take the Good News to persons living in spiritual darkness. There are however, many excuses given for not attempting to reach the lost with the gospel in a more timely fashion, but none of these will convince God, Who has given the mandate to reach those precious souls. Christ will not be content until every one of His followers are aggressively involved in the great cause of winning and discipling those perishing without hope!

John Wesley once proclaimed: "The world is my parish!," and on another occasion told his preachers in training: "Do all the good you can, By all the means you can, In all the ways you can, In all the places you can, At all the times you can, To all the souls you can, As long as ever you can."37 With this mindset, it is not hard to understand how Mr. Wesley and many of his Methodist 17th century contemporaries did so much for Christ around the world.

The evangelical Church must realize that merely preaching or singing about reaching souls for Christ is not sufficient. A.W. Tozer rebuked the lackluster Christians of his day when he wrote: "Christians do not tell lies, they just go to church and sing them." Christians getting stirred emotionally about the task of soul-winning will not get the job done. We must at some point actually do what is commanded of us. We must remind ourselves what James profoundly said; *"...be ye doers of the word, and not hearers only..."* (James 1:22) Though these words were written in the context of believing the gospel, it can apply as well to saints who should be heeding Christ's command to fulfill the Great Commission.

Jesus dealt with the matter of not being passive but active in the faith in His parable concerning the wise man and the foolish man who built their homes upon the rock and sand, respectively. Jesus said, *"Therefore whosoever heareth these sayings of mine, and doeth them, I will liken him unto a wise man, which built his house upon a rock:"* (Matthew 7:24) The truly wise person puts the words of Christ into practice: they are doers of the Word. All Christian believers should be committed to doing God's will!

Following is a light-hearted story which demonstrates the need for Christians to become active in the work of the Lord: "There was a man who told about a certain church that had what is called a Quitting Meeting. 'What is that?' someone asked out of curiosity. I had never heard of such a meeting before, but apparently, it is similar to a revival meeting. The only difference is in this meeting the people are called on to quit certain things: quit drinking alcohol, quit smoking tobacco, quit cursing, etc. One elderly lady went forward during the invitation time. The preacher asked her why she came forward, because he and everybody else knew that she had been a godly person for most of her long life. She replied, "I have not been doing anything, and I am quitting!"38 So it should be with each of us. If we have been doing no serving and little good for the Lord during our Christian life, then we need to quit and start doing something! The next chapter will explain the various areas in which Christians should be involved while endeavoring to fulfill the Great Commission.

The service we do for our Master must begin at 'home,' as Paul wrote to the Galatian believers: *"And let us not be weary in well doing: for in due season we shall reap, if we faint not. As we have therefore opportunity, let us do good unto all men, especially unto them who are of the household of faith."* (Galatians 6:8-9). After serving locally, however, may we not forget that our service for the Lord must also extend beyond the Church, that is -globally.

The Apostle Paul wrote to the church in Rome: *"I am debtor both to the Greeks, and to the Barbarians; both to the wise, and to the unwise. So, as much as in me is, I am ready to preach the gospel..."* (Romans 1:14-15a) Paul's desire was to serve his fellow Christians, but he also had a burning passion to tell the heathen about the wonderful love and salvation of Jesus Christ. Listen to the burdened Apostle's words: *"Yea, so have I strived to preach the gospel, not where Christ was named, lest I should build upon another man's foundation: But as it is written, To whom he was not spoken of, they shall see: and they that have not heard shall understand."* (Romans 15:20-21) Verse 21 is a reference to Isaiah 52:15, the passage upon which this book is named-*The Sprinkle of Nations.*

It is obvious that Paul was not content to merely minister among the well harvested fields of his day. He wanted to go the extra mile and labor for Christ in the least reached lands. As you may recall, *The Macedonian Call* (Acts 16:9) was a call to action. Paul was already a missionary, but having received a special call with specific directions, he responded with assertive action, not apathy, no matter what it may cost him.

The great scientist, Louis Pasteur, is quoted as saying, "In what way can I be of service to humanity? My time and energy belong to mankind." In a sense, this was Paul's attitude as well and should be that of all Christians who have in their possession the spiritual medicine that all of mankind so desperately needs!

Since the days of the early church, there has always been a direct correlation between revival and the Church's interest in working for God in missions. The day of Pentecost provided Christ's disciples with power to be witnesses for Him (Acts 1:8). The Baptism of the Holy Ghost was given so that Christians might be empowered to be a witness for Christ and His gospel, by means of both preaching and suffering.

The infilling of the Holy Ghost provided all that Christ's followers needed to serve Him. They received a mind for purity of doctrine, for piety in life, for perseverance through suffering, and a heart full of passion for souls. Acts 8:4 declares *"Therefore they that were scattered abroad went every where preaching the word."* The word preaching here can be translated *"euaggelizo,"* or evangelizing. The Baptism of the Holy Ghost turned the early Church into a group of fiery evangelists who longed to tell others about the saving grace of Jesus Christ. Noted Bible scholar Albert Barnes comments on this event by stating: "It is not said that they set themselves up for public teachers; or that they administered baptism; or that they founded churches; but they proclaimed everywhere the news that a Savior had come. Their hearts were full of it. Out of the abundance of the heart the mouth speaks; and they made the truth known to all they met."39

There is an erroneous belief concerning revival in some churches today which promotes the idea that the Holy Ghost is given so that the believer can have happiness and a good feeling. Though this is partially true, what makes this belief so dangerous is that it places all the emphasis on feeling and little or none on working for God in His harvest fields.

A careful study of the major revivals in Church history proves that true revival causes the revitalized Church to become not only pure in its doctrine and lifestyle, but passionate in its duty to the Master by obeying the Great Commission. The following is one account that should cause all Christians today to yearn for a repeat of these past days. "As a direct result of the Azusa Street outpouring, thousands of individuals were led into a deeper relationship with Jesus Christ. People began to study the Word of God, become convicted of sin, and surrender their lives to Christ. They were baptized with the Holy Ghost, Who led them into greater spiritual truths found in the Word of God. The Spirit of God empowered them with boldness to fulfill the Master's mandate for missions (Matthew 28:18-20)

Signs and wonders followed those who believed, such as blinded eyes being opened, deaf being able to hear, mute being able to speak, the lame made to walk, and the dead raised to life again. Such reports are commonplace among these early Pentecostal believers, and all of these signs testify of the glory and power of the risen Christ. The early Spirit-filled believers considered everyone to be witnesses, and many sailed to foreign lands to share the gospel message.

This move of God at Azusa Street was not only for Los Angeles, but it was designed for the whole world—even future generations. What happened there has helped renew Christianity, bringing fresh vision and passion to the Great Commission. Consumed with zeal for God and empowered by the Holy Spirit, individuals have taken the Word of God to diverse villages and races across the globe. As a result many have learned of the love and grace of Christ, ultimately preparing the world for His return."40

Instead of being idle, indifferent or insignificant, God wants His people to be industrious for Him. The power of the Holy Ghost is available to assist all believers in being just that. The Apostle wrote: *"And whatsoever ye do, do it heartily, as to the Lord, and not unto men;"* (Colossians 3:23) Not everyone can be an Apostle Paul or a David Livingstone; but we all can be our best, and that is what God is asking of us.

The following story should stir and hopefully inspire every saint of God to become a more active laborer in the harvest of souls. Ed Spencer was attending Northwestern

University at Evanston, Illinois. Ed was a rather well known athlete of his day, for he was one of the first to win a gold medal for the United States in the Olympics. The campus of Northwestern is bordered on one side by Lake Michigan. One evening, as Ed was doing his studies in the library, outside a storm was raging. All of a sudden some fellows came running in shouting, "The Lady Elgin has just been thrown in the rocks and is sinking." Ed ran from the library out to the lake and saw the situation was indeed serious. Without a moment's hesitation, he rid himself of any extra clothing that might hinder him and be dived in the rolling, chopping waves. He was able to reach the wreck and, fighting his way back, he brought the first person to safety. He had repeated this heroic effort several more times when those on shore said, "Ed, you have done all you can. You will surely kill yourself if you try it anymore." Ed's reply was, "I have got to do my best." He plunged again and brought another one to safety, and another and another until he had rescued 17 people. He could go no further and fell unconscious on shore. All through the night, as he lay in the infirmary, he kept repeating, "Have I done my best, fellows? Fellows, have I done my best?" He had done his best but the experience cost him his health. Years later, inspired by the story, Ensign Edwin Young wrote the song, "Have I Done My Best For Jesus?"

"I wonder, have I done my best for Jesus,
Who died upon the cruel tree?
To think of His great sacrifice at Calvary!
I know my Lord expects the best from me."

31 C. Gordon Olson; *What in the World is God Doing?;* p. 85
32 The Problem of Self; Gene Taylor
33, 34, 35 PowerBible CD
36 www.believers-chapel.org
37 John Wesley's Rules
38 Steve Shepherd, sermon
39 PowerBible CD
40 www.azusastreet100.net

Part Three
¥

The Commitment to Missions

CHARLES PAHLMAN D. MIN.

Introduction:

In his book on Christian missions, J.P. Barrett wrote: "...the missionary spirit first lived in the great heart of God- it budded and blossomed and fruited in His love, constraining Him to give His priceless possession, His Son, for the salvation of man."[41] The salvation of any soul is entirely dependent upon God's willingness to save. Had God chosen to deal with fallen humanity in the same manner in which He dealt with sinful angels (Jude 1:6), absolutely none could be saved and enjoy eternal life with Christ in heaven.

God's unconditional love is the driving force behind His desire to save the sinner. John 3:16 is possibly the most widely known verse in the Bible: *"For God so loved the world, that he gave his only begotten Son, that whosoever believeth in him should not perish, but have everlasting life."* This verse does not mean that all men will be saved, but that all have the opportunity to be redeemed because God loves them enough to provide His Son as a sacrifice for their sin. The Triune God is fully committed to saving lost humanity from its dreadful plight, and it only seems reasonable that His followers should be committed to the same great cause!

In his book entitled *The Militant Moderate*, John Holcomb wittingly writes: "You must get involved to have an impact. No one is impressed with the won-lost record of the referee."[42] In order for the gospel to have its greatest possible impact, all Christians must become fully committed to world missions. Though I desire not to sound critical, I must say that the term *involved* is still not sufficient when considering reaching the world for Christ. To merely be involved in an activity is different than being fully committed to it. As an example, consider the following humorous illustration: "With regard to ham and eggs: The chicken is involved; the pig, committed."[43]

Many sincere Christians seem comfortable with doing "a little" for the cause of Christ around the world. This statement begs the question, "Was this the attitude of the early Christians described in the book of Acts?" It should be pointed out that this New Testament book is our model for how the Church of today should operate. Denominations and Christian fellowships attempt to model their church government after the example set forth in the book of Acts. Classical Pentecostals, such as I, strongly affirm that this exciting book written by Luke sets the precedent for our doctrinal stances on the gifts of the Holy Ghost, sanctification, signs and wonders, etc. Therefore, this historical, yet relevant book must remain our guide as well in the matter of world missions and the evangelization of the lost. We must not forget that after the disciples received the baptism of the Holy Ghost, they became world wide "missionaries." (Acts 1:8) We should be asking ourselves, "Is that my desire as well?"

J. Oswald Smith wrote: "So many of us are localized in our outlook. We see only our own community, our own village or town, and we never see beyond. There are those who think only of their own church and have no interest in what others are doing. Then there are some who have a larger vision. They see an entire city or province and they are ready to give their money and to work for its evangelization. But they, too, are local in their outlook, for they never see beyond the boundaries of the city or province in which they live. Then there are those who have a still larger vision. They see an entire country and they are ready to work for its evangelization. But even they are local in their outlook, for they never see beyond the boundaries of the country in which they live. Then there are those, however, who still have a larger vision. They see a continent and they are ready to do all they can for the evangelization of their continent. Yet even they are local in their outlook for they never see beyond the boundaries of their continent. Then there are those who see an entire world. They see Europe, Asia, Africa, North and South America and the Islands of the Seas. They have God's vision and that is the vision he wants us to have, a world vision."44 We must remember that Jesus Christ has done all He can for us, now we must do all we can for Him.

Please consider carefully the message of this story: "There is a legend told concerning the return of Jesus to Heaven. Meeting Gabriel, He stated that He had completed His divinely appointed task. 'And what is your plan?'

enquired Gabriel. 'How is the Gospel to be spread? Did you leave a strong organization on the earth with well defined plans?' 'No,' answered the Savior. 'I left no organization, only a small company of disciples, mostly of very humble birth. They are to tell the world.' 'But suppose they fail you,' persisted Gabriel. 'What plan have you then?' 'I have no other,' replied the Savior, sorrowfully!"

Let us be reminded of the serious warning in Ezekiel 3:18; "*When I say unto the wicked, Thou shalt surely die; and thou givest him not warning, nor speakest to warn the wicked from his wicked way, to save his life; the same wicked man shall die in his iniquity; but his blood will I require at thine hand.*"

Multitudes will someday march by the throne of judgment, pointing an accusing finger of scorn at burden-less saints and crying "No man cared for my soul!" Some of those same Christians will attempt to justify themselves by exclaiming, "But, Lord, am I my brother's keeper?" God's answer could well be, "The voice of thy brother's blood crieth unto me from Africa, from China, from the islands of the sea." *The voice of thy brother's blood.* Christian friend, please keep in mind that it is no light thing to be a watchman. "His blood will I require at thine hand." The supreme task of the church is the evangelization of the world, and all who claim to be a part of that church must commit themselves totally to the fulfillment of that mandate and responsibility.

41 JP Barrett; Fruit Bearing Truths, p. 61
42 The Militant Moderate, John Holcomb; 1991
43 HeavenWord Illustrations
44 J. Oswald Smith; The Passion for Souls; Marshall, Morgan, and Scott; London; p. 26

Chapter Five

~

Commit to Supporting

We generally consider the term commitment to mean giving one's all to some cause or some person. I am reminded of an article I read concerning members of a particular religious Cult. The article stated: "In Salt Lake City, in the downtown mall, between Radio Shack and B. Dalton Books, there is a unique shop: a Mormon missionary supply store. It provides young missionaries with everything they need to prepare for a mission to another country. They have T-shirts with the designated country's flag, brochures, books that give tips for packing, and just about anything else."45

Although you will not likely find a store like this in your hometown, this report clearly reminds us how totally committed many Mormons are to the task of spreading their deceptive and dangerous doctrine.

To show just how dedicated some of these cult members are, note the following facts which are taken from a valid website discussing Mormonism:

- Mormon missionaries give up 1.5 to 2 years of their lives for full time missionary service
- Mormon missionaries are generally between the ages of 19 and 25
- Mormon missionaries are not paid for any of their services (in fact, they pay their own fees) 46

In a similar way, concerning commitment to a cause, someone asserted: "Corporations are willing to invest more for marketing their product than Christians are for sending the Gospel. In 1986, Coca-Cola claimed that 97% of the world had heard of their product, 72% had seen it, and 51% had tasted it."47 The writer went on to state: "When Christians make a similar commitment to spreading the Gospel as Coke has done to market their product, then we can expect to see a dramatic increase in mission outreach."48

The poignant yet real statistics concerning missions

giving among today's Evangelicals should call us to take drastic action. Though a bit dated, the following report is alarming: "Churchgoers are donating an increasingly smaller share of their incomes. The percentage of income Protestants give fell from 3.1 in 1968 to 2.5 in 1998, according to Empty Tomb, a research group in Champaign, IL. That means church members gave $4 billion less in 1998 than they would have if they were giving at the same rate they did in 1968. Total annual contributions rose by an average of $202 to $570 per church member, after inflation was taken into account, because incomes also rose. ...Most of the money is being spent on salaries, in-church programs, and building-maintenance rather than on outreach efforts such as missions and services for the poor. Donations for external church activities dropped to a 30-year low as a percentage of income, falling below .04 percent, according to the study. Gifts to support local congregations represented 2.2 percent of church members' income in 1998."[49]

In an article entitled Are We Trifling with Missions; A.B. Simpson, founder of the Christian Missionary Alliance wrote: "I am a little afraid that the seeds of a great apostasy are in the Church of God today, that in the midst of this century and its closing decade it should even be questioned whether we could evangelize the world in our generation, when the luxuries alone that crowd our homes, that cover our persons, that are hung upon our walls and stuffed into our library cases, the gold and silver, the jewelry and the ornamentation, the costly furniture in our homes, would of themselves suffice to make the Gospel speed its way around the earth inside of a decade of years."[50] These are especially alarming words when we take into consideration that this was written over 100 years ago.

Of course God is not calling all Christians to live like a recluse or pauper. He has not commanded us to give up all the comforts and opulence that we enjoy in the prosperous, civilized world in which many of us find ourselves. However, the Lord does desire for His disciples to put Him and His cause first in their lives, which always includes giving of their substance to the Lord's work. Carefully notice the truth in Paul's words to the

Corinthians: "For if there be first a willing mind, it is accepted according to that a man hath, and not according to that he hath not." (2 Corinthians 8:12) God is not expecting us to give what we do not have, but rather to give faithfully and generously from what we do have. We must ask ourselves this important question, "Where did we get our abilities and our possessions?" The answer is "From God, of course!" Paul states it this way: "...and what hast thou that thou didst not receive? now if thou didst receive it." (1 Corinthians 4:7)

The Lord has entrusted us with treasures and talents for the main purpose of glorifying Him and doing His will and work. The following Scripture can be applied to all Christians, not just the nation of Israel: "But thou shalt remember the LORD thy God: for it is he that giveth thee power to get wealth, that he may establish his covenant which he sware unto thy fathers, as it is this day" (Deuteronomy 8:18) The Family Note Commentary records on this truth: "Power to get wealth, and also liberty to keep and enjoy it, are from the Lord. For this reason it should ever be viewed as his gift, and employed in promoting His cause."[51]

Paul commended and praised some Christians of His day for their generosity, but likewise rebuked those who were selfish and would not share of their means to help reach others with the truth (read 2 Corinthians, chapter 9). Amy Carmichael, Irish missionary to India, well stated, "You can give without loving. But you cannot love without giving." [52]

If it is true that souls without Christ are headed for hell, and if it is correct that the only way they can escape eternal judgment is to believe the gospel of Jesus Christ, then it only makes sense that the right thing for Christians to do is to generously support the cause of spreading the gospel to the lost with our money and resources.

The story is told of the day General William Booth, founder of the Salvation Army, was asked to meet with Queen Victoria of England. Because she had heard so many favorable things about his work in the slums, she asked him for the secret of his success. "Your Majesty," he replied,

"Some men have a passion for money. Some people have a passion for things. I have a passion for people."

If we truly love God and His kingdom as we say we do, we will, as is sometimes quoted "put our money where our mouth is." According to 1 Timothy 6: 9-10, those who love money are idolaters and, in reality, are doing much harm to themselves by their covetous ways.

Though humorous, the following illustration brings to light a problem with which a growing number of Christians struggle: "Every time a man said the word 'money,' he insisted on repeating it three times. When one day he said to his wife, 'Give me some money, money, money and I will buy some groceries,' his family suggested he consult a psychiatrist. 'You are uptight about money,' explained the psychiatrist. 'You need to replace that fear with a stronger emotion. Every time you say the word love, repeat it three times. That will help you get over your problem with money.' 'What a terrific idea!' said the man. 'If there is anything I love, love, love, it is money, money, money.'" Instead of things or money, we are to love God supreme and our neighbor as ourselves, just as Jesus taught us to do (Matthew 22:37-38).

In a spiritual sense, loving our neighbor means not just supplying their physical needs when they are in material want, but more importantly, supplying their spiritual need by giving them a chance to hear the gospel of Christ before they perish eternally.

The reality is, far too many Christians are bound by materialism and the desire for passing pleasures. Many members of God's family hoard His money and refuse to give to the only cause that will last forever. Scores of God's people have debts and other financial constraints brought about by a desire to have more of this world. Having material things is not a sin: the problem begins when things "have you!" The wise man said, *"The rich ruleth over the poor, and the borrower is servant to the lender."* (Proverbs 22:7).

Ajith Fernando, the prominent evangelical leader from Sri Lanka, made the following statement in an interview with Mission Frontiers magazine in September of 2001: "The Great Commission deals with such an absolutely urgent issue that we should be willing to die for it! Giving (finances) is just a small part of that dying!"53 Each of us who have received the gospel has done so at the expense of someone else. So then, can we not give of ourselves and our substance that others may hear the Good News as well? If giving means "dying," in a sense, then let us "die" so that others may live.

John Wesley, the Christian leader of the seventeenth century, gave a sound biblical approach to Christian stewardship when he wrote the following: "Christians are to 'do good.' *'As we have therefore opportunity, let us do good unto all men, especially unto them who are of the household of faith'* (Galatians 6:10). After the Christian has provided for the family, the creditors, and the business, the next obligation is to use any money that is left to meet the needs of others."54 Wesley recognized some situations were not clear-cut. He accordingly offered four questions to help his hearers:

1. In spending this money, am I acting like I own it, or am I acting like the Lord's trustee?

2. What Scripture requires me to spend this money in this way?

3. Can I offer up this purchase as a sacrifice to the Lord?

4. Will God reward me for this expenditure at the resurrection of the just?' 55

These Scriptural principles transcend all time, and are useful for every generation. The Lord desires to help each of us to be good and faithful stewards of our possessions, using them to glorify Himself by supporting those who are reaching sinners for Christ.

At this point, it is helpful to discuss the *why* and the *how* of World Missions support. When studying the matter from a theological standpoint, one will discover that there are several main philosophies. These viewpoints differ mostly based on the outcome of the support, or more simply, how the monies are distributed and used.

Scripture clearly teaches what the goal of missions should be. Mission work's key objectives are: Exalt Christ, Evangelize the Christ-less (the lost), and Establish Churches, which helps disciple those won to Christ in their particular nation. Simply stated, the method of the Apostle Paul, a model missionary for all New Testament believers, was to establish Indigenous Churches. This means that every established Church should eventually become:

1. self-supporting; 2. self-governing; 3. self-propagating.

These three points, known as the *"3 Self's of Missionary Work"* were well articulated by two missionary men of the past several centuries, they are: Henry Venn (1796 - 1873) and Rufus Anderson (1796 - 1880)

One modern Christian source states: "Melvin Hodges (1909-1988), an Assemblies of God missionary to Nicaragua, again popularized the idea in the 1950s with his book, *On the Mission Field: The Indigenous Church*. He defined the indigenous church as 'a native church . . . which shares the life of the country in which it is planted and finds itself ready to govern itself, support itself, and reproduce itself.' Hodges believed that foreign money creates dependence and establishes paternalistic patterns within mission movements, leading to an unhealthy, anemic church.... He emphasized the need for flexibility and tailoring the principles to fit the need of the local believers."[56]

Two books on this subject have been masterfully written by Roland Allen: *Missionary Methods: St. Paul's or Ours?* (1912) and *The Spontaneous Expansion of the Church: And Causes that Hinder It*. These classic works would assist any who has the desire to know more on this missionary subject.

In discussing what makes a church *Indigenous*, I wish to make clear that we must be careful concerning criticism of how another carries out their particular missions work for Christ. Depending on various factors, (i.e. cultural norms) in a particular nation, the obtaining of the *Three Self* ideals may not be easily achieved. For a period of time, or possibly forever, the *Three Selfs* may be unbalanced. For example, the missionary and sending agency may find it easier to guide a national pastor and church into becoming self- governing than into becoming self-supporting, or vice versa. In some cases, one or more of the *Three Selfs* may not be fully developed, depending on the customs and traditions of the people group. Again, we must beware not to wrongfully critique missionaries who are implementing and practicing the *Three Self* method differently than we would.

Without compromising Scriptural truth, each situation must be judged on its own particulars. It may take a generation or more to help a people group to understand the concepts of the *three-self* model. Patience, persistence and most of all prayer will be essential in this endeavor to teach a nation how to become self-supporting, self-governing, and self-propagating.

A proper understanding of *contextualization*, explaining the gospel in such a way that the people of another culture can understand, will be of great benefit in bringing about an indigenous church in foreign lands. The following statement found in *The Willowbank Report* confirms this fact:

"Sensitive cross-cultural witnesses will not arrive at their sphere of service with a pre-packaged gospel. They must have a clear grasp of the 'given' truth of the gospel. But they will fail to communicate successfully if they try to impose this on people without reference to their own cultural situation and that of the people to whom they go. It is only by active, loving engagement with the local people, thinking in their thought patterns, understanding their world-view, listening to their questions, and feeling their burdens, that the whole believing community (of which the missionary is a part) will be able to respond to their need. By common prayer, thought and heart-searching, in dependence on the Holy Spirit, expatriate and local believers may learn together how to present Christ and contextualize the gospel with an equal degree of faithfulness and relevance. We are not claiming that it will be easy, although some Third World cultures have a natural affinity to biblical culture. But we believe that fresh creative understandings do emerge when the Spirit-led believing community is listening and reacting sensitively to both the truth of Scripture and the needs of the world."[57]

It is correct to say that the "*three-self*" model is not totally sufficient in and of itself, and an indigenous Church is not fully defined by such relatively broad terms. However, the model is still a useful in encouraging high ideals.

I personally believe that as long as the Word of God is not being compromised, there must be the freedom on the part of the missionary and the sending agency to pragmatically, ethically, and yet wisely strive to win and disciple souls for Christ. May we ever remember that our vision is to enable missionaries to focus unhindered on their calling according to Matthew 28:19.

Missionary and consulting director of Overseas Missionary Fellowship J. Oswald Sanders gives sound advice on this subject when he explains: "One of the acid tests of missionary leadership is willingness to delegate responsibility to emerging national leaders the moment they evidence sufficient spiritual maturity and then to stand by, ready to help, while they gain experience in the same way as the missionary did, by trial and error. ... In the earlier stages, a wise watchfulness will be necessary, but a resort to interference should be made only if the need becomes acute. The sense of being watched destroys confidence."[58]

Regarding the financial support of World Missions, there are some important questions that should be asked by every missions supporting church and sending agency. They are as follows:

1) Should the 'givers' take on the responsibility of knowing that their offering will be used to teach and practice correct biblical doctrine?

The answer is a commanding 'Yes!' The New Testament teaches responsible missionary giving. (1 Cor. 16:1-3, 2 Cor. 8:18-23, 2 Cor. 9:12-13, Titus 2:1-15.) Sadly, some ministers believe that 'faith-giving' is giving with no responsibility. But, as 'faith' to give comes from the Word of God (1 Cor. 10:15) so the receiver of that offering should be responsible to obey the Word of God.

2) What methods of missionary giving contradict the Biblical principles?

The answer in part is that giving support without requiring accountability contradicts the Bible principle. Missionaries must try to always assure their supporters that they teach sound doctrine and try to encourage their supporters by keeping them informed of the work being done. (1Cor. 9.16; 2 Cor. 10:1-18, Phil. 4.)

A foreign Church that receives support for its Pastor or its projects should practice accountability to the giver concerning its message, methods, and money. This accountability is needed to edify the Church. Missionaries should teach mission pastors and churches that financial help from outside should be a temporary substitute, and challenge them toward full and independent responsibility. (2 Corinthians 12:13.) Albert Barnes comments about Paul's attitude concerning churches contributing to their own support: "It is a privilege to contribute to the support of the gospel, and they who are permitted to do it should esteem themselves highly favored."59

Many churches and agencies send missionaries to remote areas to bring the gospel to nations who would otherwise never hear the plan of salvation. While this is perfectly in line with Jesus' commandment, these missionaries often find themselves in financially dismal situations. A new culture, foreign environment and a lack of proper communication with the locals is tough enough, but also having to struggle financially is overwhelming to the missionary and crippling to the purpose.

The responsibility of those staying behind is to support these missionary workers not just in prayer, but in finances as well. God could, but probably will not, simply let money fall out of heaven. He wants us to be the instruments that provide funding to keep these faithful gospel workers and their families going.

The act of giving to God's work around the world should never be a drudgery or merely a duty, but a delight. Paul wrote along these lines when he said *"... He which soweth sparingly shall reap also sparingly;.... Every man according as he purposeth in his heart, so let him give; not grudgingly, or of necessity: for God loveth a cheerful giver."* 2 Corinthians 9:6-7

Those who are fully in love with Christ will love what He loves, and we know that He loves souls. Love is active, and God demonstrated His love by giving; He gave His only begotten Son Jesus Christ (John 3:16). We, too, demonstrate our love by giving back to God of all that we have, including our money. We give cheerfully because we delight to please Him who ransomed us, but also because we love souls and realize that money is needed to help rescue them from sin and hell. We should be thrilled to be a part of God's plan of mercy, grace and love!

Randy Alcorn, a Christian author wrote in his book *The Treasure Principle*: "Recently I was attending a gathering of givers. We went around the room and told our stories. The words fun, joy, exciting, and wonderful kept surfacing. There were lots of smiles and laughter, along with tears of joy. One older couple eagerly shared how they are always traveling around the world, getting involved in the ministries they support and are giving to. Meanwhile, their home in the states is becoming rundown. They said, "Our children keep telling us, 'Fix up your house or buy a new one. You can afford it!' We tell them, 'Why should we do that? That is not what excites us!'"[60]

We all realize there is nothing wrong with fixing up one's house or even buying a new one. However, this story illustrates how a devoted disciple of Christ really feels regarding the most important work in the world, that of winning souls and building up the Kingdom of God. Nothing is more exhilarating or rewarding than this!

45 Heaven Word Illustrations
46 www.aboutmormonism.com
47 www.sermonillustrations.com
48 Ibid
49 John Mark Ministries
50 www.missionfrontiers.org
51 Power Bible CD; FBN- Deut. 8:18.
52 www.snu.edu Missions Slogans
53 www.missionfrontiers.org; Sept. 2001
54 Dr. Charles Edward White; Leadership Magazine (Spring Arbor College, Michigan); 1987
55 Ibid
56 Internet Article: "Indigenous church mission theory".
57 Lausanne Committee for World Evangelization; 1978
58 J. Oswald Sanders , Spiritual Leadership, ; p. 171
59 PowerBible CD. Barnes Notes
60 Randy Alcorn; The Treasure Principle; Multnomah Publishers; Sisters, OR; 2001; pp 26-27

Chapter Six

~

Commit to Going

Financial giving fills a great need in the work of God, both locally and globally. However, monetary funding is only one need in God's kingdom; there is also the need for those who will go. Giving to world missions is commendable, but someone must actually take the gospel message to those in spiritual darkness.

Going with the gospel message is at the very heart of Jesus' charge to his followers, as these following verses illustrate:

Matthew 28:19 *"Go ye therefore, and teach all nations, baptizing them in the name of the Father, and of the Son, and of the Holy Ghost"*:

Mark 16:15 *"And he said unto them, Go ye into all the world, and preach the gospel to every creature."*

John 20:21 *"Then said Jesus to them again, Peace be unto you: as my Father hath sent me, even so send I you."*

Romans 10:14 *"How then shall they call on him in whom they have not believed? and how shall they believe in him of whom they have not heard? and how shall they hear without a preacher?"*

2 Corinthians 4:3 *"But if our gospel be hid, it is hid to them that are lost:"*

Many in the Evangelical and Protestant Church profess to believe the Bible, but then struggle with or simply refuse to live out the mandates of the very Scripture they claim to embrace. It is ones actions, not words, that will ultimately tell the truth about what they truly believe. If we believe the Bible, we will obey its commands. Motivational speaker Charlotte Roberts has wisely stated: "There is a distinction between our 'espoused' values -- which we profess to believe in -- and our 'values in action,' which actually guide our behavior."[61] It is not enough to only believe what is right; we must engage it and make it our own by practicing what we profess.

One of the clearest yet most neglected mandates in all of the Word of God concerns getting involved in world evangelization. Someone wrote: "Go, send, or disobey."62 The following commentary illustrates the sad neglect today of Jesus' mandate to go:

"Most people today do not believe in the cause of foreign missions. Walbert Buhlmann, a Catholic missions secretary in Rome, speaks for many mainline denominational leaders when he says, 'In the past we had the so-called motive of saving souls. We were convinced that if not baptized, people in the masses would go to hell. Now, thanks be to God, we believe that all people and all religions are already living in the grace and love of God and will be saved by God's mercy.' (Time Magazine, Dec. 27, 1982, p.52). Sister Emmanuelle of Cairo, Egypt, says, 'Today we do not talk about conversion any more. We talk about being friends. My job is to prove that God is love and to bring courage to these people.' Many today, like these two Roman Catholic missionary leaders, do not submit themselves to the authority of God in the Bible, but instead create their own God according to what they would like Him to say. Since they would like him to say that all men are saved whether they hear the gospel of Christ or not, therefore that is the kind of God they create." Unfortunately, this is a modern form of idolatry; making God who they desire Him to be; sadder yet, this mind set is taking hold even in the Evangelical church world.

The following statement is telling and troubling: "LifeWay Research, associated with the Southern Baptist Convention, found that two out of 10 Evangelicals... agreed with the statement that eternal life can be obtained through religions other than Christianity."63 Though the 20% of Evangelicals who embraced a view of Universalism seems like a small number, it is the leaven that will grow if not halted by those with the truth. It is certain that if we who have God's Truth do not take it to those in spiritual darkness, they will eternally perish! If we neglect this global mandate from our Master Jesus Christ, are we not, in a sense, in a deceived condition similar to the Roman Catholic ministers mentioned previously? It is understandable that not every Christian has the ability or the call to leave home and actually go to a foreign land as a missionary. The basic method of worldwide evangelism and missions is this:

1) someone must go;   2) someone must send.

It is the responsibility of every Bible believing Christian to either go or to send someone in their place, for this is the only way worldwide evangelization will be accomplished. The question then arises for each of us: "Which choice will I make?" Sadly, many Christians today have little interest in seeing the gospel message propagated even in their own city, let alone in a foreign land. Though this sounds harsh, we must at some point, for our own good, be forced to face the facts. The true state of a church is revealed when the following questions are honestly answered:

- How many in the church attempt to win souls?
- How many pray for missionaries?
- How many give generously to support world missions?

If, when these questions are asked, we find ourselves wanting, we should be driven to our knees and motivated to action. When convicted of neglecting our responsibility to win the lost, either at home or abroad, may we respond like Isaiah, who immediately repented of his dereliction of duty. Upon his repentance, Isaiah wholly volunteered himself to God's work crying *"Here am I (Lord), send me!"* (Isaiah 6:8) Spurgeon remarks about Isaiah's surrendering prayer: "When a man's lips have felt the sacrificial flame, he is bold to go upon the Lord's errands, as though it were to the world's end."[64] Though there are some who neglect the call to go or send others as missionaries, the good news is that God is still raising up an "army" of zealous Christian "soldiers" for these last days. Scott Moreau, chair of intercultural studies at Wheaton College (Illinois) stated, "The day of Western missionary dominance is over, not because Western missionaries have died off, but because the rest of the world has caught the vision and is engaged and energized." If we are too busy building our own "little kingdom" to help build God's kingdom, the Lord will still find a way to get His work completed. I have personally been in nations such as Nigeria, the Philippines, Honduras and Burma (Myanmar) where the majority of the people, including Christians, are extremely poor. Christian persecution is intense in some of these areas, yet many of these believers still have a burning desire to spread the gospel. I will highlight several of these works and their leaders in a subsequent chapter.

On the surface, this fact seems confusing: the churches and Christians with the greatest resources appear to be doing the least evangelistic work. I realize that there are many believers doing their best to spread the gospel to the nations, and their efforts are praiseworthy. However, God needs even more Christians just like them. I am challenged myself as I write this book, for I see my own need to become more involved in fulfilling the greatest task that the Master left to His church: *The Great Commission.*

The apathy of some, revealed by their lack of involvement and 'going' for the cause Christ, reminds me of this story:

"Luiqi Tarisio was found dead one morning with hardly any personal comforts in his home, except the presence of 246 exquisite violins. He had been collecting them all of his life. They were all stored in the attic, the best in the bottom drawer of an old rickety bureau. In his very devotion to the violin, he had robbed the world of all that music. Much of that collection was owned by others before him who had done the same. When the greatest of his collection, a Stradivarius, was first played, it had sat silent for 147 years."[65]

After that account, we must ask ourselves: how many of Christ's people are like old Tarisio? In our love for God's church, we fail to give His glad tidings to the world: in our zeal for the truth, we fail to publish it. When shall we learn that the Gospel does not just need to be cherished, but also shared? Lest Christians believe that this talk is too radical or overbearing, take the time to consider the thoughts of an American minister whose passion is expressed in this song that he wrote over a century ago:

The Regions Beyond

To the regions beyond I must go, I must go
Where the story has never been told;
To the millions that never have heard of His love,
I must tell the sweet story of old.

Refrain:
To the regions beyond I must go, I must go,
Till the world, all the world,
His salvation shall know.

To the hardest of places He calls me to go,
Never thinking of comfort or ease;
The world may pronounce me a dreamer, a fool,
Enough if the Master I please.

Oh, you that are spending your leisure and powers
In those pleasures so foolish and fond;
Awake from your selfishness, folly and sin,
And go to the regions beyond.

There are other "lost sheep" that the Master must bring,
And to them must the message be told;
He sends me to gather them out of all lands,
And welcome them back to His fold. - A.B. Simpson

These challenging yet inspiring words come from a man who caught the vision of what it means to fulfill the Great Commission. Albert Benjamin Simpson became one of the greatest missionary leaders of our modern era. During his ministry, he helped create the Christian Missionary Alliance and launched America's first illustrated missionary magazine, *The Gospel in All Lands*. In his local church, Simpson's creative passion for missions gave birth to what local churches now call *Faith Promise Conventions*.

Long and Short term Missions:

In order to solve some of the problems in the church regarding missionary work, it is necessary to clearly define terms used and objectives given. Some Christians and even pastors have what I like to call a "missionary phobia," while others in the Church struggle with apathy or just sheer boredom with the whole subject of missions.

Christians often forget that mission work is not a solo effort, but a matter of team work. As earlier stated, not all are called to go overseas as a long term missionary or even as a short-term worker on a foreign field. However, when God's children fall in love with the 'Lord of the Harvest,' they notice that what matters most is simply doing the part that they have been called to in the work of God's harvest field.

The old maxim says, "A house divided will fall." There is no room for jealousy or envy among the workers in God's harvest, for if these attitudes prevail, the cause of missions will be greatly hindered. We are a spiritual body, with each member being given our particular function. In order for the Body of Christ to be healthy, its members must appreciate one another, along with each individual's gifts and calling. D.L. Moody profoundly stated: "There are two ways of being united -- one is by being frozen together, and the other is by being melted together. What Christians need is to be united in brotherly love, and then they may expect to have power."[66]

A superb expositional study of the vital subject of Christian unity is found in 1 Corinthians 12. Here, Paul discusses the diversity of gifts and ministry callings, but argues that all saints must share the same spirit of love and grace which will result in a spirit of unity. One commentator explains Paul's words as follows: "Here gifts are ascribed to the Holy Ghost, administrations to the Lord Christ, and operations to God the Father; but in all these there are great diversities both of kinds and degrees; they differ in their nature, extent, and use. Thus it is with reference to spiritual gifts: but in the case of sanctifying graces it was far otherwise; these are all bestowed jointly, or not at all."[67]

As believers in Christ, the reality of our missions responsibility is that we are all missionaries. According to the Bible, all Christians are commissioned to reach the lost with the gospel, to be "fishers of men." No one can catch fish while sitting at home. I recognize that not all Christians are capable of leaving their home to evangelize, but there is little excuse for making no attempt whatsoever to reach the lost. I have been made aware of saints who made use of their pen, telephone, or computer to share their faith in Jesus. It has been well said that "As a Christian, you are either a missionary or a mission field!" In his letter to the Corinthian church, Paul reminded the believers there that Christ *"...hath given to us (believers) the ministry of reconciliation;"* and because of that calling, he referred to all Christians as *"ambassadors for Christ."* Adam Clarke describes Paul's use of the word ambassador in this way: "Ambassador is a person sent from one sovereign power to another; and is supposed to represent the person of the sovereign by whom he is deputed."68

Though every Christian has a general calling to be an ambassador for Christ, each one has their own specific area in which they are to witness and labor for Him. In the early church, there were Christians such as Paul and Barnabas who were destined to go to the uttermost parts of the earth to spread the gospel message. At the same time, the saints who remained in Israel to preach were not criticized for doing so. The main concern was they were faithful to their calling in the place where God had planted them. These followers of Christ were not competing with others working in a different area of the world, but were supportive of each other and held each other accountable for the work they were doing. (see- Acts 15)

The entire Christian family should be stirred to action by a genuine compassion for those in spiritual darkness. Kurt von Schleicher said: "Our God of Grace often gives us a second chance, but there is no second chance to harvest a ripe crop."69 We must care enough to make an effort to send the message, whether we take it personally, or help to send someone else. Missionary Pastor J. Oswald Smith rightly stated it this way: "I must go, or send a substitute."70

Different Types of Missions Work

It is important to make a distinction between the ministry callings which the Lord gives to individuals. Knowing that there are various gifts and callings, will help believers to work together as a team for the good of all. World Missions work can be divided basically into two broad categories, Long Term and Short Term. These categorizations in no way exhaust the many varieties of missions work, but I use these two divisions because I believe they are most relevant to the popular understanding of mission work in today's church world.

Prior to defining long and short term missions, I think that it would be beneficial to define the basic term 'Missions.' The modern view of mission work has been somewhat oversimplified. Some are comfortable with stating that Missions only means the churches' endeavor to reach souls for Christ. Though this is true, it does not begin to explain the wide spectrum of responsibilities and activities involved in the world of mission work.

In my opinion, an excellent and more articulate definition of Missions is given by C. Gordon Olson who declares: "Missions is the whole task, endeavor, and program of the Church of Jesus Christ to reach out across geographical and or cultural boundaries by sending missionaries to evangelize people who have never heard or who have little opportunity to hear the saving gospel."[71] Mr. Olson's description of Missions should help us to better understand the meaning and mandate behind effective Christian Missions.

Long-Term Workers:

The International Mission Board defined a long term missionary: "A long-term missionary.... is a person who responds to God's call and gifting to leave his or her comfort zone, cross geographical, cultural, or other barriers to proclaim the gospel and live out a Christian witness in obedience to the Great Commission."[72] The inference is that their work is a lengthy endeavor, possibly lasting a life time.

Obviously, long term mission work is no light matter. The price that these men and women and families pay is often enormous. Consider the following words spoken by a key note speaker at a recent convention for retiring full-time missionaries: "You did not go to the mission field seeking an affluent lifestyle or a comfortable living; you did not go and persevere until retirement because of an affluent pension that awaited you,' said IMB president Jerry Rankin. 'Many years ago you had to come to the point of realizing 'it is not about my joy; it is not about my success; it is not about my personal fulfillment.' 'You have given your life as a living sacrifice to the Lord,' he said."73

Long term missionaries are a unique group indeed, for they not only have a calling to this kind of work, but equally have a conviction about it. This conviction can be partly summarized by the following statement made by the Nazarene founder and missionary leader P.F. Bresee; "We are debtors to every man to give him the gospel in the same measure in which we have received it."74 The call and conviction work together to bring about a commitment that keeps them laboring on, even in the toughest of circumstances.

No sacrifice is too great for these faithful and zealous laborers for the Lord. William Borden (1887-1913) turned his back on comfort, affluence and position when he chose to go to the foreign field as a young man. Borden never made it to the mission field however, for he died on his way. One writer briefly describes Borden's life as follows; "'Although he was a millionaire, Bill seemed to realize always that he must be about his Father's business, and not wasting time in the pursuit of amusement.' Although Borden refused to join a fraternity at Yale, 'he did more with his classmates in his senior year than ever before.' He presided over the huge student missionary conference held at Yale and served as president of the honor society Phi Beta Kappa.

Upon graduation, Borden turned down some high paying job offers..... William Borden went on to graduate work at Princeton Seminary in New Jersey. When he finished his studies at Princeton, he sailed for China. Because he was hoping to work with Muslims, he stopped first in Egypt to study Arabic. While there, he contracted spinal meningitis. Within a month, 25-year-old William Borden was dead.... 'Was Borden's untimely death a waste?' asked the writer. 'Not in God's plan.' Prior to his death, Borden had written the following words in his Bible.....'No reserves,' and 'No retreats,' 'No regrets.'"75

Borden's life story and motto have impacted and inspired many Christians for the cause of Christ and World Missions. The motto Borden inscribed in his Bible, *"No reserves, No retreats, No regrets"* expresses what I believe to be the very heart and soul of all genuinely spiritual long-term missionaries.

It is no secret that there is an ongoing need for more long-term missionary workers in our day. One leading missionary leader recently stated: "Long-term workers are the best hope that many of the world's most unreached people have of spending an eternity with God. They demonstrate through words and actions the love God has for the people among whom they work. They can see a level of fruitfulness that only comes from a long-term connection with an unreached people."76 Another writes, "Career missionaries are the foundation of our mission efforts. They invest a lifetime in cross-cultural evangelism, church development, and church planting movements.... They are gifted at using their professional, vocational, technical, and ministerial skills to share the gospel and lead the lost to Christ, which is our primary goal and purpose."77

In reality, long term missionaries are not only preachers, but may as well be involved in some of the following areas: Church-planting, Community development, Discipling, or acting as Doctors, Evangelists, Health care workers, Nurses, Schoolteachers, Team administrators, and Team leaders. For some, using these professions may be the only way they are able to enter a particular country due to laws that oppose the Christian gospel and its workers. No matter what profession the missionary employs on the foreign field, the over-arching goal of all missionaries is to lead people to Christ.

The support of these missionaries by the 'home' church is critical. Even one faithful missionary forced to return from the field due to a lack of resources is one too many. We must keep these dedicated volunteers on the 'front lines' of evangelism and church planting by our faithful support. The following was compiled by Stephen Ross, and is a suggested list of things the local homes churches can do to help support faithful and dedicated long term missionaries:

- Have a well-written missions policy.
- Have a functioning missions committee.
- Have a faith promise giving program.
- Have men's and women's groups focus on missions.
- Have a missionary couple/family to lead Vacation Bible School.
- Have visiting missionaries speak in the Christian school chapel and Bible class.
- Provide lodging during the summer for MK's (missionary kids) attending Christian college and help them find summer jobs.
- Provide housing and transportation for missionaries on furlough.
- Give generously to visiting missionaries
- Help the visiting missionary with maintaining their automobile, etc.
- Maintain a missionary "closet" of good used clothing, etc. for visiting missionaries on furlough.
- Organize a missions trip for interested church members and school students.
- Send a construction team to help a missionary with a project on the field.
- Have a section of the Sunday bulletin dedicated to missions (a quote by a missionary, statistics, etc.)
- Pray regularly for your missionaries.
- Communicate regularly with the missionaries the church supports.
- Encourage young persons to be pen pals with missionary children of their own age.
- Have a church missions bulletin board where prayer letters, etc. are posted and where there is a world map indicating location of the missionaries...
- Make missionary biographies available for purchase or for lending from a church resource table.

- Have an annual missions conference.
- Pastoral leadership (preaching on missions, public invitations to surrender to full-time Christian service, using stories relating to missions as sermon illustrations, etc.).[78]

Short-Term Workers:

According to Missiologist C. Gordon Olson, there are roughly 2500 Protestant Missionary organizations and that number is rapidly expanding. One of the fastest growing segments is the area of short term ministries.

A good description of short term missions work is as follows: "Short-term mission has always been set apart from career or long-term mission by the distinction of time. But how much time?—Two weeks? Two months? Two years? That is subjective, and best determined on a case-by-case basis with a given sending entity and receiving field. A better definition would still encompass time, but rather than prescribing a fixed number of weeks or months or years, would use the term 'temporary.' A better definition would also add the terms 'swift' and 'volunteer' to more accurately describe what short-term mission really is."[79] Though this is not a new concept in missions, it is becoming more popular.

The following statistics given by a prominent missions agency in the U.S. give an idea how big the short term movement has become: "In 1965 student researcher Thomas Chandler noted only 540 individuals from North America involved in short-term mission. In 1989 an estimate by a Fuller School of World Mission doctoral student put the number at 120,000. Three years later it had more than doubled to 250,000. By 1998 Evangelical Fellowship of Mission Agencies (EFMA) vice president and former InterVarsity Mission Urbana director John Kyle's research put the figure at 450,000. In 2003 Peterson, Aeschliman and Sneed estimated at least one million short-termers were being sent out from a globally-sent perspective each year. In 2004, Robert Priest, director of the doctoral program in Intercultural Studies at Trinity Evangelical Divinity School, reported he was beginning to locate data suggesting the number could be as high as four million." 80

Some factors which may influence the rising interest in short-term missions are ease of travel and a growing awareness of the need for mission work around the world due to better means of communication.

Some may question the value of short-term missions work because of the expense and effort in paying for, planning and maintaining such a trip. Others may argue that this time and money would be better spent in aiding the missionaries already on the field. Roger Peterson, CEO of STEM International, one of the leading short-term mission agencies in the world, answers these objections and concerns by briefly saying: "Short-term mission can be a bona fide (and perhaps the best) missiological strategy when the field need is for swift, temporary, non-professional volunteers." 81

Concerning the benefits of short-term missions work, Lee Primeau, a Pentecostal church leader in Canada remarks: "In our existential society, people want to experience first hand what God is doing through the church globally in order to connect and develop passion for the lost. Second, the local church is able to nurture an ongoing relationship with a community of believers in another part of the world. Third, it helps people consider the part they play in reaching the lost over a longer term. For example, it could be a young person exploring his or her future or an adult considering where to invest his or her time, money and energy in the second half of life. Many return from a short-term mission trip committed to missions. Fourth, the local church benefits when returning STM'ers reinvest their expertise and passion to share the love of Christ in their home church."82

Having traveled to the mission field over twenty-five times, I can say from experience that it has been what I call a 'win-win situation' every time. Though most trips have had their difficulties and even disappointments, these were minor in comparison to what was gained. When a short-term missions team has the right attitude, has their trip well organized, and maintains clear communication between the team leader(s) and the long-term missionaries, the short-term effort becomes a great blessing and success. The majority of testimonials from both short-term workers and long-term missionaries confirm this fact.

Following are first hand reports from several students and a faculty member of Free Gospel Bible Institute, a school that sent mission teams to the Philippines, India, Nigeria, and Honduras. *S.E.N.T Ministries* (Student Evangelism to the Nations Teams), is a ministry I initiated 2005.

Amber Galiher (Missouri)- "What an amazing opportunity I was handed when I was selected to go to the other side of the world! There were times when the only response to what I saw or felt was to cry. God did amazing things while we were there, but some how while I was ministering, I was ministered to. I have had the chance to see life through another's eyes and see what it is really like to be a missionary."

James Burgess (California)- "This has been a wonderful experience. This week I have had the opportunity to minister in ways that I never dreamed I would get to minister. It was amazing to see what God will do when you step out of your comfort zone and into His will. We did that, He took over, and the rest is history."

Mercy Schultz Bruce (Ohio)- "I will never forget this trip, and how it has changed my perspective on life and the world in which we live.... I have been challenged to put more effort into preparing for the long-term ministry that God has called me to."

Vijay Malhar (Bombay, India)- "This mission trip has stirred me up so much that now my prayer is "Lord, use me as you wish in any field, any land, among any people." Ministry is not only behind the pulpit preaching, but it is also out on the foreign field. This mission trip has increased my burden for missions. All I pray now is "Lord please use me at any cost," and my cry is 'Lord give me souls, else I die!"

Claire (Beam) Goodwin (Texas)-
(*former FGBI faculty*)
"We have lifted up our eyes and looked on the fields and will never be the same. The ripened harvest is great and the laborers are few.....And words cannot describe the excitement and thrill of being able to materially help so many. You should have seen the looks of shock and awe when so many realized what gifts were being given to them.

The SENT Team painting the interior of a Filipino Free Gospel Church

(l-r):
Vanessa Miller,
JoAnna Brady,
Mercy Schultz, &
Heather Nietzel
in Manila

Trynda Peyton (Arkansas)- "I want to thank the Lord for the opportunity to return to the Philippine Islands. It was such a blessing to see the hunger for God. My eyes were truly opened to the needs across the world. I was touched, stirred, and changed."

Michael and LuAnn Petit-

(Missionaries to The Philippines)- It has been our privilege to be blessed by the ministry of the SENT team for the past two years. Their selfless ministry has really challenged the lives of the Faith Bible Institute students, Free Gospel Church pastors, and others, including my wife and I. The outpouring of their love by making provision for these people's material needs speaks volumes to everyone concerning their sincere desire to help. The SENT team has been a real asset to this mission field."

Andrew Goodwin (Texas) India 2008: "All of my life I have heard stories told by missionaries, of the great need of the lost across the world. But until this missions trip it was just a story or picture in my mind's eye. What was once just a thought has now become a reality...I know that I will never be able to look at missions the same again.

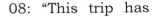

Shavanna Taylor (Kentucky)- India 08: "This trip has caused me to realize that I cannot allow my fears to keep me from doing something for God...my prayer is that it was not me that they saw, but that they have seen Christ in me; for it means nothing if they remember my name, but that they may know the name of Christ."

Ashley Peyton (Arkansas)- India 2007-2008: "I will always remember this mission trips...I know beyond a shadow of a doubt that God had placed a burden on my heart for missions. This trip has changed my life forever! As a result of this trip, I wrote a song entitled:

"Will You Be The One" - The chorus says:
Are you willing to be the one to say 'you can use me.'
I'll carry the truth where ever You may lead.
Are you willing to be the one to leave behind all you've known. The voice of God is calling to you...
"Will you be the one?"

Cole Perkins (Lawton, OK) Honduras- 2010

"My perspective... has completely changed! I've learned that it takes more than a burden for ministry to make a missionary, but one must fall in love with the people also..."

Sonia Vargas (Indiana) Nigeria 2010: "This trip to Nigeria has challenged and motivated me. I've never met a people who have hardly anything materially to give, yet they do so with such a joy, love and sincerity. It made me examine myself even more so."

Ashley Rosson (FGBI faculty)

Nigeria & India: "Thank you so much for giving us this opportunity with the SENT missions program....it has changed my life forever...!"

The setting and enforcement of standards is a vital part of preparing Christians for short-term missions work, whether they are to aid in a spiritual and educational way, or to assist in building and repairing physical structures. Next is a list of team standards compiled by SOE Ministries:

Standard#1: GOD-CENTEREDNESS
An excellent short-term mission seeks first God's glory and his kingdom, and is expressed through our:

Purpose — Centering on God's glory and His ends throughout our entire STM process.

Lives — Sound biblical doctrine, persistent prayer, and godliness in all our thoughts, words, and deeds.

Methods — Wise, biblical, and culturally-appropriate methods which bear spiritual fruit.

Standard #2: EMPOWERING PARTNERSHIPS
An excellent short-term mission establishes healthy, interdependent, on-going relationships between sending and receiving partners, and is expressed by:

Primary focus on intended receptors
Plans which benefit all participants
Mutual trust and accountability

Standard #3: MUTUAL DESIGN
An excellent short-term mission collaboratively plans each specific outreach for the benefit of all participants, and is expressed by:

On-field methods and activities aligned to long-term strategies of the partnership.
Goer-guests' ability to implement their part of the plan.
Host receivers' ability to implement their part of the plan

Standard #4: COMPREHENSIVE ADMINISTRATION
An excellent short-term mission exhibits integrity through reliable set-up and thorough administration for all participants, and is expressed by:
Truthfulness in promotion, finances, and reporting results
Appropriate risk management
Quality program delivery and support logistics

Standard #5: QUALIFIED LEADERSHIP
An excellent short-term mission screens, trains, and develops capable leadership for all participants, and is expressed by:
 Character — Spiritually mature servant leadership
 Skills — Prepared, competent, organized, and accountable leadership
 Values — Empowering and equipping leadership

Standard #6: APPROPRIATE TRAINING
An excellent short-term mission prepares and equips all participants for the mutually designed outreach, and is expressed by:
Biblical, appropriate, and timely training
On-going training and equipping (pre-field, on-field, post-field)
Qualified trainers

Standard #7: THOROUGH FOLLOW-UP
An excellent short-term mission assures debriefing and appropriate follow-up for all participants, and is expressed by:

 Comprehensive debriefing (pre, on, & post-field)
 On-field re-entry preparation
 Post-field follow-up and evaluation

61	www.digently-seeking-god.com; Apr 6.
62	www.snu.edu. John Piper quote
63	Christian Post; Jennifer Riley; July 5, 2008
64	Power Bible CD; Spurgeon's Commentary
65	James S. Hewett, Illustrations Unlimited, Wheaton: Tyndale, 1988
66	www.sermonillustrations.com; Unity
67	www.sermonillustrations.com; Unity
68	Power Bible CD; W. Burkitt, on 1 Cor. 12.
69	Power Bible CD; Adam Clarke; on 2 Cor. 5:20
70	www.snu.edu; Missions Quotes
71	Ibid
72	C. Gordon Olson; pg. 13
73	International Mission Board website
74	Ibid
75	www.snu.edu; Missionary Quotes
76	www.snu.edu; Missionary Stories
77	Baptist General conference
78	Ibid
79	www.wholesomewords.com
80	www.lausanneworldplus.com/perpectives
81	www.lausanneworldplus.com/perpectives
82	Ibid
83	www.christianity.ca/mission/global
84	www.mission2go.com/Adventure/Finder/Articles

Chapter Seven

~

Commit to Praying

Paul, the eminent missionary and Apostle of the early church, knew very well that the work of missions will never succeed unless there is a complete dependence upon God. He wrote to fellow believers at Corinth the following: *"Not that we are sufficient of ourselves to think any thing as of ourselves; but our sufficiency is of God;... Who also hath made us able ministers of the new testament;"* (2Corinthians 3:5-6) One commentary explains: "He would claim no credit for the work at Corinth, as though it was his own, for all his strength was of God."[84] Prior to His departure from this world, Jesus told His disciples: *"I am the vine, ye are the branches: He that abideth in me, and I in him, the same bringeth forth much fruit: for without me ye can do nothing."* (John 15:5) Other verses could be cited along with this one which reminds believers that God's work can only be accomplished through trust and dependence upon Him. The virtue of full dependence on God will only become evident in our lives and ministries through much time spent in earnest prayer.

Wesley Duewel, the head of OMS ministries said: "We can reach our world, if we will. The greatest lack today is not people or funds. The greatest need is prayer." Samuel Zwemer; the early 1900's American missionary leader to the Islamic world once wrote: "The history of missions is the history of answered prayer." When praying for God's work and His kingdom, Christians often struggle with such things as the lack of a heart felt burden, wandering thoughts, and praying broad, general prayers such as 'Lord save the lost around the world,' or 'Lord help all the missionaries.' These problems tend to hinder Christians from praying effectively for legitimate missions work both at home and abroad.

One of the first steps in overcoming these troubles is to view prayer in a much more serious manner than many today generally do. Speaking of the critical nature of prayer,

J. Oswald Smith said: "Intercessory prayer is the Christian's most effective weapon. Nothing can withstand its power. It will do things when all else has failed. And the marvel is that we turn to other agencies in order to accomplish what only prayer can bring to pass. God has placed this mighty weapon in our hands, and He expects us to use it. How disappointed He must be when we lay it aside and substitute natural means for supernatural work."[85]

A serious *attitude* toward prayer must first be revived in our churches, but it naturally follows that we then must develop a *method* of prayer. Jesus gave a model for prayer in both Matthew's and Luke's gospel (Matthew 6:9-11; Luke 11:2-4). We often refer to this passage as The Lord's Prayer, but in reality, it is Jesus' own example to us of how we should pray. In my judgment, a basic outline of prayer for missions work includes the following two categories: Prayer for Self and Prayer for Others.

Prayer for Self:

Jesus made it clear that everyone who follows Him must be willing to deny all else in order to do so (Mark 8:34). When Isaiah saw the Lord in a vision in the temple (Isaiah 6), notice that he did not recommend anyone else for service to the Lord, but said, *"Here am I Lord, send ME!"*

A prayer to the Lord of the harvest for laborers includes first and foremost the volunteering of one's self for the job. Consider the passion in the words of the African missionary Robert Moffat: "Oh, that I had a thousand lives, and a thousand bodies! All of them should be devoted to no other employment but to preach Christ to these degraded, despised, yet beloved mortals."[86] It is this kind of prayer that God honors. Reason reminds us that not everyone can go to the mission field, but the passionate soul winner desires to see someone go to the heathen if they cannot, and will support those who go with all of their efforts, including prayer.

Regrettably, many believers do not pray much about missions work for fear of themselves or a loved one being called to go to a foreign field. To help Christians overcome these qualms, we who have the true gospel should honestly ask ourselves the following questions:

1. Why is there such a shortage of workers for overseas work?

2. Why does there exist such a disproportionate number of workers here at home compared to those laboring in the most needy areas?

The missionary Isabel Kohn once stated: "I believe that in each generation God has called enough men and women to evangelize all the yet unreached tribes of the earth.... It is not God who does not call. It is man who will not respond!" 87 Each one of us must prayerfully discover the unique role to which He has called us in the task of reaching this generation for Christ!

The sure way to eliminate excuses for not being more involved in mission work is for Christians to die out to self. In Romans 12:1 Paul charges: *"I beseech you therefore, brethren, by the mercies of God, that ye present your bodies a living sacrifice, holy, acceptable unto God, which is your reasonable service."* When we love our lives more than we love the Lord and perishing souls, many will suffer as a result of our selfishness. Death to self is a must if we are to be healthy and effective Christians.

When James Calvert set out as a missionary to the cannibals of the Fiji Islands, the ship captain tried to turn him back, saying, "You will lose your life and the lives of those with you if you go among such savages." To that, Calvert replied, "We died before we came here."88

Due to a rise in prosperity and "creature comforts," the average Western Christian today knows little about self sacrifice, which is precisely what the propagation of the gospel is based upon. Roderick Davis said "Love is the root of missions; sacrifice is the fruit of missions." 89 We must constantly remind ourselves that Jesus gave His all, and He now requires that His followers do the same.

The task of praying for missions begins with this kind of prayer: *"Lord, what wilt Thou have me to do!"* (Acts 9:6) Paul offered this prayer at the time of his conversion. Why then, is it so difficult for those who have been saved

CHARLES PAHLMAN D. MIN.

for a much longer period of time to pray this same kind of prayer?

The next prayer that we as Christ's followers should offer is simply this: *"...nevertheless not my will, but thine, be done."* (Luke 22:42). God's answer to the first prayer will inform us concerning what He wants us to do individually. However, being informed without being transformed will result in frustration and futility. Receiving God's instructions for our life does not guarantee that we will do what He commands. It is we who must make ourselves ready to do God's perfect will, which will only be accomplished as we surrender our will to His. We must put "feet" to our prayers. God's work, regardless where it is, involves both knowing and doing.

The following quote from C.T. Studd may seem a bit harsh, but I believe this type of exhortation is necessary in order to arouse Christians who offer vain excuses for doing little or nothing for God. "We Christians too often substitute prayer for playing the game. Prayer is good; but when used as a substitute for obedience, it is nothing but a blatant hypocrisy, a despicable Pharisaism...To your knees, man! And to your Bible! Decide at once! Do not hedge! Time flies! Cease your insults to God, quit consulting flesh and blood. Stop your lame, lying, and cowardly excuses. Enlist!"[90]

Though carrying out God's work may seem intimidating at times, it always leads to peace of heart and mind. In over twenty years of ministry, I have visited several areas of the world which are considered dangerous. Others, concerned for my safety, have attempted to persuade me not to go. I encouraged myself, however, with the fact that God's perfect will is the safest place in the world to be. The knowledge that God had opened the door for me to go and proclaim His Word calmed any fears and concerns I may have experienced. Andrew Murray once wrote, "God is ready to assume full responsibility for the life wholly yielded to Him."[91] Our Father has the whole world in His hands, so let us who are His children not be afraid to offer ourselves in prayer and service to Him, no matter where He may take us!

- 94 -

Prayer for Others:

In order to do missions work effectively, we must have an intercessory prayer life. Such prayer involves praying for:

I). The Laborers- Praying for Missionaries

One of the most common questions Christians ask regarding missionaries is, "How can I pray for missionaries?" Here are a few suggestions given by one missionary organization on how to pray:

1. Select at least one of the missionaries your church supports and pray for their relationship with God. We often assume too much in this area, having placed all missionaries on a high pedestal marked Super-Spiritual Saint. It may not occur to us that missionaries have needs regarding their walk with God. On behalf of your missionary, pray for him or her in these areas:

      a.   Feeding on God's Word
      b.   Prayer life
      c.   Maturity and growth in grace
      d.   Victory over Satan and the flesh

2. Pray for your missionary's physical and emotional life. Many missionaries live and work in difficult climates where various diseases are prevalent. Pray for their health and safety, as well as for deliverance from discouragement, loneliness and depression when they are in the thick of a spiritual battle.

3. Pray for your missionary's family. If they are married, pray for their marital relationship. Pray for the children's salvation and growth in the Lord. Pray that, as a family, they will provide an excellent model among the people they serve.

4. Pray for your missionary's ability to communicate. Communication is a foundational key to all mission work. Missionaries must communicate with both their life and lips. For many, they must adapt to a new culture and learn a foreign language. Many languages are difficult to learn, and a superficial knowledge of the language makes communicating a spiritual truth extremely challenging.

Besides knowing the language, a missionary must adapt culturally and communicate the love of Christ to the people he or she is seeking to reach, which can be a daunting task at times.

5. Pray for your missionary's ministry. Support your missionary in what they are doing: witnessing, visiting, teaching, preaching, or whatever they do to serve the Lord. Their letters posted on the missionary bulletin board in the church will give you lots of ammunition for prayer. Pray for boldness, open doors and open hearts.

6. Pray for your missionary's fellow workers. Your missionary is most likely not ministering completely alone, but is part of a team working closely with the believers in that country. Often in these situations, Satan works overtime to get into these working relationships and cause strife and disunity.

7. Pray for your missionary's country of service. Include in your prayers the entire country where your missionaries are. Pray for a climate of responsiveness to the gospel.

I highly recommend *Operation World* by Patrick Johnstone as one of the best guides available in praying for all the countries of the world.

Using this information, we are left without excuse for not praying for our godly missionaries. Let this be a challenge for all of us to choose at least one missionary with whom we will get involved: read their letters, write to them, and pray for them consistently. Remember the words of Jesus: *"Men ought always to pray and not to faint."* (Luke 18:1)

Let us not forget that all Christians, especially leaders and missionaries, are engaged in spiritual warfare, and prayer is one of the chief weapons God has given to us to counter Satan's assaults. The following story illustrates the need to be constantly in prayer for missionaries who often find themselves in extremely difficult circumstances:

"A Christian leader named Steve --was traveling recently by airplane. He noticed that the man sitting two seats over was thumbing through some little cards and moving his lips. The man looked professorial with his goatee and graying brown hair, and Steve placed him at fifty-something. Guessing the man was a fellow-believer, Steve leaned over to engage him in conversation. 'Looks to me like you are memorizing something,' he said. 'No, actually I was praying,' the man said. Steve introduced himself. 'I believe in prayer too,' he said. 'Well, I have a specific assignment,' said the man with the goatee. 'What is that?' Steve asked. 'I am praying for the downfall of Christian pastors.' 'I would certainly fit into that category,' Steve said. 'Is my name on the list?' 'Not on my list,' the man replied."92 Though I cannot personally verify the 100% accuracy of this account, it well illustrates the underlying principle that Satan and his workers are dedicated to the destruction of God's work and God's people! If the enemy is working this feverishly, should not the church be likewise doing all it can to be effective in winning souls and building up God's kingdom?

Unfortunately, many Christians underestimate the power and effectiveness of prayer. If we constantly remind ourselves that God's work stands or falls on prayer, I am convinced that we will do much more of it. If we fail to truly believe in the power of prayer, and do not practice a life of prayer, we will no doubt experience a power shortage in our own life and ministry.

The story is told of a particular seminary missions class in which Herbert Jackson, a new missionary, was assigned a car that would not start without a push. After pondering the problem, he devised a plan. He went to a school near his home and received permission to take a few children out of class and had them push his car off. As he made his rounds, he would either park on a hill or leave the engine running. He used this ingenious procedure for two years. Ill health forced the Jackson family to leave, and a new missionary came to that station. When Jackson proudly began to explain his arrangement for getting the car started, the new man began looking under the hood. Before the explanation was complete, the new missionary interrupted, "Why, Dr. Jackson, I believe the only trouble is this loose cable." He gave the cable a twist, stepped into the car, pushed the switch, and to Jackson's astonishment, the engine roared to life.

For two years needless trouble had become routine. The power was there all the time. Only a loose connection kept Jackson from putting that power to work. God's power is always available to mission workers; we can have it if we will learn to properly pray.

II). The Lost

Another important area of prayer regarding missionary work is that of interceding for lost souls around the world. J. Oswald Smith believes this to be one of the most neglected Christian disciplines, and several decades ago wrote these challenging words: "In this twentieth century we are, more and more, turning from the God-appointed means of intercessory prayer and adopting, instead, merely natural agencies for the carrying on of His work. Everywhere we look it is the same, both in evangelism and ordinary church work. Intercessory prayer has been shelved. For some reason it is out of date. Our methods, we say, are better, our plans more successful, and so we adopt natural means to bring to pass the supernatural."[93]

If we are to be scripturally sound saints, we must constantly remind ourselves to be regularly engaged in intercessory prayer. Paul wrote to Timothy and said: *"I exhort therefore, that, first of all, supplications, prayers, intercessions, and giving of thanks, be made for all men; For kings, and for all that are in authority;.... For this is good and acceptable in the sight of God our Savior; Who will have all men to be saved, and to come unto the knowledge of the truth."* (1 Timothy 2:1-4) One commentator suggests: "This points out a sometimes forgotten aspect about praying for the lost - that governments can do a lot to help or to hinder the process of evangelism. For instance in Albania, one of the world's most atheistic communist states a generation of people has been raised without the remotest awareness of Jesus Christ or the gospel. Albania is in ruins as a result and is without the social services or human compassion that the influence of the gospel brings. On the other hand Samoa and some of the Pacific nations are very Christian and the Government actively encourages participation in Christian activities. Everyone has some knowledge of the gospel and many are saved....God wants 'all people everywhere' - that means the lot of you without exception - to pray for those in authority so that we may openly have permission to preach the gospel without hindrance."94

The task of intercessory prayer seems daunting at times, but the matter is too important to give up on. We must begin somewhere, and must allow our burden to increase in the matter of praying for the lost.

The following guide may be a helpful when praying for lost souls. It is taken from a booklet entitled *Love on It's Knees* by Dick Eastman who suggests that Christians: "Pray that God would cause these people (lost) to ask certain 'heart' questions that will direct their thinking toward the things of God.

- Whom Can I Trust?
  Plant in the hearts of the lost a skepticism about the lies they hear, whether philosophical, social, or political.
  Cause them to begin to question whom they can really trust in life.
  They would look for someone to trust beyond themselves.
  That political leaders would do things that will cause distrust.

- What is My Purpose?
  That souls will search for life's meaning.
  Plant in their hearts an urgency concerning this question.

- When Will I Really Be Free?
  Plant in the hearts of the lost an inner unrest, together with a longing to know the Truth that will someday set them free.
  That they will feel an emptiness that can only be satisfied by receiving Jesus into their lives.
  Cause them to ask, "When will I be free of this emptiness in my heart?"

- Why Do People Hate Religion or Reject God?
  Cause lost souls to question why their leaders so vehemently reject the existence of God.
  Question why people find it necessary to fight the concept of God.

- Where Will I Go When I Die?
  That God would turn this question into a quest for an eternal answer.
  Plant in their hearts a longing to resolve this issue.
  That an urgency will fill their hearts concerning their eternal state.

The knowledge of these prayer points is helpful, but will do little good if we are not motivated to pray in the first place. Praying for the lost is both a matter of the head (knowledge) and of the heart (a burden). The Psalmist said: *"They that sow in tears shall reap in joy. He that goeth forth and weepeth, bearing precious seed, shall doubtless come again with rejoicing, bringing his sheaves with him."* (Psalm 126:5-6) The original interpretation of this verse does not necessarily refer to the act of praying for the lost, but the principle set forth here well applies to prayer warriors who are passionate about interceding for those trapped in spiritual darkness. Another key verse which can be applied to intercessory prayer is Isaiah 66:7 which states: *"Before she travailed, she brought forth; before her pain came, she was delivered of a man child."*

An excellent example of intercession for the lost is Paul's passionate plea for his countrymen recorded in Romans chapter 10, verse 1: *"Brethren, my heart's desire and prayer to God for Israel is, that they might be saved."* C.H. Spurgeon made this comment about Paul's passionate plea: "The true spirit of Christianity is that of love and sympathy, it leads to prayer even for persecutors, and to hope for the most obdurate of men. Paul pleaded for the Jews."95

Jesus was the greatest example of one who poured out His soul in prayer for others who were lost. The prophet Isaiah foretold of Christ's passion for mankind: *"....because he hath poured out his soul unto death: and he was numbered with the transgressors; and he bare the sin of many, and made intercession for the transgressors."* (Isaiah 53:12)

The fulfillment of Isaiah's prophecy came in part at Calvary. Before Jesus gave up His spirit on the cross, He took time to intercede for his executioners and traitors, praying *"Father, forgive them; for they know not what they do."* (Luke 23:34). It is interesting to note, as one writer did: "God began to answer His prayer on the Day of Pentecost as some three thousand people repented and were baptized that day, and there have been countless multitudes that have been saved through the centuries."96

As Christ's followers, we must ponder our personal answers to these questions: "Do you have a heart to pray for the lost like Jesus did? Do you have the passion that inspired John Knox to plead, 'Give me Scotland or I die?' Is your attitude that of George Whitefield, who prayed, 'O Lord, give me souls or take my soul'? Do you, like Henry Martyn, mourn when you see others trapped in false religion and cry out, 'I cannot endure existence if Jesus is to be so dishonored? '"97

The seventeenth-century English Puritan Richard Baxter wrote, "Oh, if you have the hearts of Christians or of men in you, let them yearn towards your poor ignorant, ungodly neighbors. Alas, there is but a step betwixt them and death and hell; many hundred diseases are waiting ready to seize on them, and if they die unregenerate, they are lost forever. Have you hearts of rock, that cannot pity men in such a case as this? If you believe not the Word of God, and the danger of sinners, why are you Christians yourselves? If you do believe it, why do you not bestir yourself to the helping of others?"98 The *others* that Mr. Baxter speaks of refers not only to the people who are our neighbors, but to our neighboring nations as well, both near and far away. All souls are precious to God regardless of where they live. May we take to heart the words of George Bernard Shaw who wrote, "The worst sin toward our fellow creatures is not to hate them, but to be indifferent to them, that is the essence of inhumanity."99

84 Power Bible CD; PNTC; 2 Cor. 3:5.

85 Oswald J. Smith; The Work God Blesses

86 www.thebiblechannel.com

87 www.snu.edu; Missionary quotes

88 Ibid

89 www.snu.edu, missions quotes

90 Ray Comfort; The Way of the Master; Tyndale House; Wheaton, IL; p.4

91 www.sermonillustrations.com

92 Donnie Martin: The Power of Prevailing Prayer

93 Oswald J. Smith; The Work God Blesses

94 Asian Internet Bible Institute

95 Power Bible CD; SDC on Romans 10:1

96 John MacArthur; Alone With God, 1995

97 Ibid

98 D.E. Thomas, ed., A Puritan Golden Treasury; [Edinburgh: Banner of Truth, 1977], p. 92

99 George Bernard Shaw, "The Devil's Disciple- act II" (1901)

Part Four
¥
The Challenges of Missions

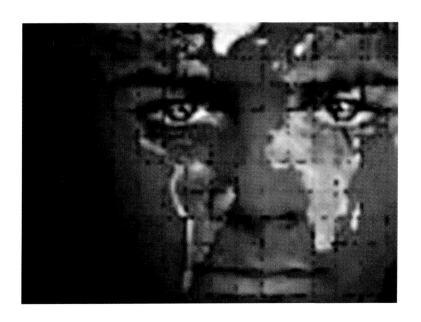

CHARLES PAHLMAN D. MIN.

From the moment man fell into sin, a great spiritual struggle on earth has taken place: the struggle of evil against good. The primary source of good is the true and living God; the source of evil is Satan. The entire conflict can be summarized in one statement of judgment given by God after man's fall: *"And I will put enmity between thee and the woman, and between thy seed and her seed; it shall bruise thy head, and thou shalt bruise his heel."* (Genesis 3:15) Arno Gaebelein comments on this grave announcement: "The words are addressed to the sinister being, the erstwhile Lucifer. Two things are prominently stated: there is to be a conflict from now on, a conflict which will go on through the ages, and in the second place the conflict will end in the bruising, or crushing, of the serpent's head. Here is the forecast of history and God's redemptive program, which will end with victory on God's side, the dethronement of evil, the defeat of lawlessness."[100]

Though Satan's kingdom will end (Romans 16:20), he continues to fight God's people and attempts to frustrate God's plan. Because of this opposition, Christians are called to arm themselves and fight Satan with the spiritual armor that God has provided based on genuine faith in God (I Peter 5:8-9); a working knowledge the Word of God (Eph. 6:17); and the Spirit of God (Romans 8:1-2; Jude 20).

Followers of Christ must keep in mind that through God they are *"more than conquerors...through Christ"* (Romans 8:37). This victory is offensive as well as defensive in nature. Simply stated, we must not only defend our salvation and God's truth (Jude 3), protecting the spiritual 'ground' that God has given to us, but must as well concentrate on taking more ground for Him and His kingdom! In the context of this book, this means we must not only protect our own souls, but must work and fight to rescue others taken captive by Satan, the enemy of God and of our souls. Abram was not content being free himself, but wanted also to rescue his nephew Lot who was overtaken by the four confederate kings.

Genesis 14:14 records the following account: *"And when Abram heard that his brother was taken captive, he armed his trained servants, born in his own house, three hundred and eighteen, and pursued them unto Dan."* This story clearly illustrates the following facts: there is a spiritual war going on, and the only way to win the war is to fight. The good news is that we do not fight alone. Thankfully, God is on our side, or rather, we are on His side! When we fight to keep our own souls as well as the souls of others, Jesus, the Captain of God's armies, helps us to be victorious.

It was courageous of Abram to take those few men and do battle with four kings, especially when they had just defeated five kings. He was daring, but not crass; he used shrewdness and wisdom by dividing his troops and attacking at night so he would win.

A valuable lesson can be learned from Abram's example. As Christian soldiers we must not only be courageous, but also seek out the wisest and most useful strategies for the battle we are engaged in. What are the strategies available to us to win the world for Christ? While we are not fighting a physical war, we are certainly fighting to save men's souls! That war, then, demands that we use every legal and legitimate means available to win this all important conflict.

Abram pursued and took on the enemy in order to save his nephew, part of his own family. We must ask ourselves: "What are we willing to do to save those around us?; "Will we engage the enemy?"; "Will we invade his kingdom?"; "Will we use good judgment in our attacks?" We cannot randomly attack and hope that victories come our way. We must carefully plan our strategy if we desire to pull souls from the clutches of sin and Satan.

In order to better understand the battle which the Church faces regarding World Missions, including the task of reaching and discipling souls, I believe we must look at the challenge from two vantage points: *The Work* and *The Workers*. These two issues were addressed by Jesus when He declared to His disciples: *"....the harvest truly is plenteous, but the laborers are few."* (Matthew 9:37)

---

100 Arno C. Gabelein D.D.; The Conflict of the Ages; Our Hope Publications; p. 31

Chapter Eight

~

The Work

"....the harvest truly is plenteous..."

The call to World Missions is a call to work. It is an important work in that it is eternal; the endeavor to reach lost souls and save them from eternal damnation. In one of his sermons concerning missions, A.W. Tozer stated the following concerning the worth of a soul: "The truth of the reality of the soul has been accepted and believed by all people and all races and all religions since time began. There are differences in the concept, but most people throughout the ages have accepted the fact that there is an essential something that lives within the inner nature of man and that the outward, physical body is only the tabernacle in which the living soul dwells.....Yes, man has a soul to save and amid all the creature noises around us, there is the still, small voice within man, saying, *"Be reconciled to God"* (2 Corinthians 5:20)."[101]

The task of missions is not only important, but also imperative. A hard look at the world around us reveals that our time to work is running out. Every minute of the hour, precious souls are perishing without the gospel. It is the imperative task of the church to get the message to those without Christ while there is still hope.

Another aspect of the work facing the Church is the fact that it is an immense task. When Jesus said that the harvest is plenteous, He was referencing the Jews and the people of Sychar of His day. Later in Matthew 13, however, He expanded the field of evangelism to that of the whole world (Matthew 13:38). He likened the world of souls to a vast field of wheat which needed to be quickly gleaned.

While it is true that our "homeland" of America is a harvest field of souls which needs to be gathered for Christ, this should not keep us who have the ability and resources to do so from gathering as well from the other parts of the harvest field. It makes no sense to keep a large number of workers concentrating on just a small portion of the field.

America and other Christianized nations have been saturated with the gospel message, while nations and people groups who have yet to hear the message of the gospel of Jesus Christ are being severely neglected. Consider what J. Oswald Smith declared in his writings: "No one has the right to hear the gospel twice, while there remains someone who has not heard it once."[102] He then boldly proclaimed that: "Any church that is not seriously involved in helping fulfill the Great Commission has forfeited its biblical right to exist."[103] This sounds like tough talk, but it is the absolute truth.

The following statistics have been provided by Jon Macon with the CHENNAI TEACHER TRAINING SCHOOL: "The United States of America has approximately 4% of the world's population and around 97% of the gospel preachers in the world. That leaves 3% of the world's gospel preachers to preach to the remaining 96% of the world's people."

The disproportionate number of Christian workers in certain parts of the world must be viewed as a real problem if it is to ever be corrected. To help us better understand the imbalance of laborers, let us ponder this enlightening parable written by James Weber, missionary to Japan.

"Once upon a time there was an apple grower who had acres and acres of apple trees. In all, he had 10,000 acres of apple orchards. One day he went to the nearby town. There, he hired 1,000 apple pickers. He told them:
'Go to my orchards. Harvest the ripe apples, and build storage buildings for them so that they will not spoil. I need to be gone for a while, but I will provide all you will need to complete the task. When I return, I will reward you for your work.

I will set up a Society for the Picking of Apples. The Society --to which you will all belong -- will be responsible for the entire operation. Naturally, in addition to those of you doing the actual harvesting, some will carry supplies, others will care for the physical needs of the group, and still others will have administrative responsibilities.

As he set up the Society structure, some people volunteered to be pickers and others to be packers. Others put their skills to work as truck drivers, cooks, accountants, storehouse builders, apple inspectors and even administrators. Every one of his workers could, of course, have picked apples. In the end, however, only 100 of the 1,000 employees wound up as full-time pickers.

The 100 pickers started harvesting immediately. Ninety-four of them began picking around the homestead. The remaining six looked out toward the horizon. They decided to head out to the far-away orchards.

Before long, the storehouses in the 800 acres immediately surrounding the homestead had been filled by the 94 pickers with beautiful, delicious apples.

The orchards on the 800 acres around the homestead had thousands of apple trees. But with almost all of the pickers concentrating on them, those trees were soon picked nearly bare. In fact, the ninety-four apple pickers working around the homestead began having difficulty finding trees which had not been picked.

As the apple picking slowed down around the homestead, Society members began channeling effort into building larger storehouses and developing better equipment for picking and packing. They even started some schools to train prospective apple pickers to replace those who one day would be too old to pick apples.

Sadly, those ninety-four pickers working around the homestead began fighting among themselves. Incredible as it may sound, some began stealing apples that had already been picked. Although there were enough trees on the 10,000 acres to keep every available worker busy, those working nearest the homestead failed to move into un-harvested areas. They just kept working those 800 acres nearest the house. Some on the northern edge sent their trucks to get apples on the southern side. And those on the south side sent their trucks to gather on the east side.

Even with all that activity, the harvest on the remaining 9,200 acres was left to just six pickers. Those six were, of course, far too few to gather all the ripe fruit in those thousands of acres. So, by the hundreds of thousands, apples rotted on the trees and fell to the ground

One of the students at the apple-picking school showed a special talent for picking apples quickly and effectively. When he heard about the thousands of acres of untouched faraway orchards, he started talking about going there.

His friends discouraged him. They said: 'Your talents and abilities make you very valuable around the homestead. You'd be wasting your talents out there. Your gifts can help us harvest apples from the trees on our central 800 acres more rapidly. That will give us more time to build bigger and better storehouses. Perhaps you could even help us devise better ways to use our big storehouses since we have wound up with more space than we need for the present crop of apples.

With so many workers and so few trees, the pickers and packers and truck drivers -- and all the rest of the Society for the Picking of Apples living around the homestead -- had time for more than just picking apples.

They built nice houses and raised their standard of living. Some became very conscious of clothing styles. Thus, when the six pickers from the far-off orchards returned to the homestead for a visit, it was apparent that they were not keeping up with the styles in vogue with the other apple pickers and packers.

To be sure, those on the homestead were always good to those six who worked in the far away orchards. When any of those six returned from the far away fields, they were given the red carpet treatment. Nonetheless, those six pickers were saddened that the Society of the

Picking of Apples spent 96 percent of its budget for bigger and better apple-picking methods and equipment and personnel for the 800 acres around the homestead while it spent only 4 percent of its budget on all those distant orchards.

To be sure, those six pickers knew that an apple is an apple wherever it may be picked. They knew that the apples around the homestead were just as important as apples far away. Still, they could not erase from their minds the sight of thousands of trees which had never been touched by a picker.

They longed for more pickers to come help them. They longed for help from packers, truck drivers, supervisors, equipment-maintenance men, and ladder builders. They wondered if the professionals working back around the homestead could teach them better apple-picking methods so that, out where they worked, fewer apples would rot and fall to the ground.

Those six sometimes wondered to themselves whether or not the Society for the Picking of Apples was doing what the orchard owner had asked it to do.

While one might question whether the Society was doing all the owner wanted done, the members did keep very busy. Several members were convinced that proper apple picking requires nothing less than the very best equipment. Thus, the Society assigned several members to develop bigger and better ladders as well as nicer boxes to store apples. The Society also prided itself at having raised the qualification level for full-time apple pickers.

When the owner returns, the Society members will crowd around him. They will proudly show off the bigger and better ladders they've built and the nice apple boxes they've designed and made. One wonders how happy that owner will be, however, when he looks out and sees the acres and acres of untouched trees with their unpicked apples."[104]

Though lengthy, this parable conveys a powerful message. Multitudes of Christians and their churches in the developed and civilized nations are paying little or no attention to the distant *orchards*. One reason offered for this apathy is a lack of knowledge concerning the severity of the situation. After teaching an intensive course on the subject of missions at a Bible institute, students came to me and stated that they had been totally unaware of the fact that so many people and nations in the world are without Bibles and the gospel message. Sadly, some even stated that they hardly ever hear of the subject of World Missions in their home church. What an alarming indictment against our modern church movement. Clearly, such churches and pastors do not fully understand their calling and role in Christ's kingdom.

I am firmly convinced that if today's Christians knew the true condition of world evangelism, more individuals would become involved in it and much more would be accomplished in the work of winning souls and training disciples for Christ. Though an accurate knowledge of the problem is only part of the solution, it is a necessary starting point. For instance, Nehemiah did not begin making plans to rebuild the walls of Jerusalem until he heard the negative report about the condition of the beloved city of God. In another case, word was sent to Peter and John concerning the need in Samaria, and upon hearing the news, they responded by going to the city to pray for and lay hands on the believers, who subsequently received the Holy Ghost (Acts 8).

In Acts chapter sixteen, Paul saw in a vision a man of Macedonia who said "Come over into Macedonia, and help us." There was a great spiritual need in Macedonia, but it was only known because it was revealed through a vision, a report of the need. It is likely that most missionary endeavors began as a result of someone hearing about the needs of a specific person or people group and responding by either going themselves or encouraging others to go. Such was the case with William Booth, founder of a ministry among the poor in the city of London, and Adoniram Judson who, after hearing of the pitiful condition of the people in Asia, was providentially directed by God to go and minister to the lost people of Burma. Irish missionary Amy Carmichael beheld in a vision the spiritually horrible plight of the heathen in India and took action to help rescue them from hell's eternal flames. Oh, that we as followers of Christ might hear the voices of the lost, see their condemned condition and be motivated to start out on a mission to save them!

I realize that Christians are needed everywhere, including in their home country. I currently pastor a Full Gospel church in Northeast, Ohio, and I feel that it is a great opportunity and privilege to shepherd the fine people whom the Lord has given me to pastor. This area of the world needs a witness for Christ. However, we as a church congregation well recognize the fact that we are called to spread the message of God's truth that He has seen fit to give us. For this reason, we support numerous missionaries with both our prayers and offerings every month. The generous financial assistance of my home church as well as others has allowed me to take many short term missions trips in an effort to make a difference in our world for Christ. We cannot do everything, but it is my conviction that we can, and should do something to reach the multitudes who sit lost in darkness.

The following story illustrates the vital need to get involved doing something for world missions, even though it may seem small and insignificant:

"A well known author and poet was working and vacationing on the southern coast of Spain. One morning, very early, he was walking along the beach. The sun was just rising, the rain had ended, the rainbows were magnificent, the sea calm. While enjoying the beauty about him, he glanced down the beach and saw a lone figure dancing about.

Fascinated by this other person celebrating the day that was to dawn, he moved closer. As he came nearer, he realized that the young man was not dancing, but in one graceful movement was picking objects up from off the beach and tossing them into the sea. As he approached the young man, he saw that the objects were starfish. 'Why in the world are you throwing starfish into the water?' he asked. 'If the starfish are still on the beach when the tide goes out and the sun rises higher in the sky, they will die,' replied the young man as he continued tossing them out to sea. 'That is ridiculous! There are thousands of miles of beach and millions of starfish. You cannot really believe that what you are doing could possibly make a difference.' The young man picked up another starfish, paused thoughtfully and remarked as he tossed it out into the waves, 'It makes a difference to this one.' "[105]

Thankfully, there are a growing number of pastors, evangelists, and churches getting involved in making a difference around the world for Christ. I attribute this growth largely to the increased amount of information available concerning the spiritual condition of the lost. Missionaries and missions agencies are beginning to reach more spiritually deprived areas and are able to bring first hand reports of the needs there. As the message spreads, so does the burden for these unreached people. The Spirit of God can then prompt individuals to do their part to meet the need.

Certain missionary organizations today are doing a supreme job of identifying the areas of the world in greatest need of hearing the gospel. There are many false ministers who travel the world preaching a counterfeit gospel. Knowing this, it is urgent that we reach people with the true message of salvation in Jesus Christ before they are deceived by the false doctrines being touted.

In recent decades, major cults such as the Mormons, Jehovah's Witnesses, and the New Age movement have won many converts to their cause. Sadly, the enemy has blinded millions of souls by leading them into mere religiosity in place of a personal relationship with Jesus Christ. Multitudes of nominal Christians attend church but have never been born again according to the Biblical standard of John 3. Roman Catholics are an example of this, seeking salvation through their church, the Virgin Mary or by a priest. Self-righteous Protestants are no better off if they trust in a salvation by good works instead of a personal faith in Jesus Christ.

In addition to those who trust in religion alone to save them, millions claim to have no belief system at all, such as secular humanists, agnostics, and atheists. These all need to be evangelized with the gospel of Jesus Christ. Truly, the mission fields are plenteous and diverse!

The area of the world known for having the greatest need of the gospel has been called "The 10/40 Window." A simple and adequate definition for this term is: "The 10/40 Window is an area of the world that contains the largest population of non-Christians in the world. The area extends from 10 degrees to 40 degrees North of the equator, and stretches from North Africa across to China."106

> *"The bedrock of missions is not the value of man, it is the spread of God's glory. the biblical commitment to evangelism and missions is rooted in God's passionate concern to make His name known."* ~ Steve Fernandez

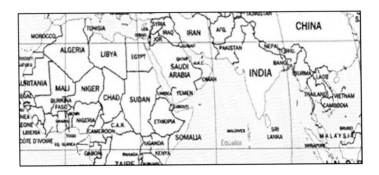

The 10/40 Window

The following information, provided by *The 10/40 Window Ministry,* highlights the great needs of the people who live within this geographical zone of the world:

1) The Physical Need . . .

...There are over 400 mega cities (cities with more than 1 million people) in the world today. 300 of these cities lie within the Window.
...The Window contains the majority of the world's least evangelized mega cities. Of the top 50 cities on this list, all 50 cities are in the 10/40 Window
...More than 97% of the poorest of the poor live in the Window.
...On average, people living in the 10/40 Window exist on less than $500 per person per year.

2) The Spiritual Need . . .

...71 % of all Muslims, 98 % of all Hindus, and 68% of all Buddhists live in the 10/40 Window.
...There are 34 Muslims countries, 7 Buddhist nations, 3 Marxist nations and 2 Hindu countries in the Window.
...There are 55 countries in the world that are considered "Unevangelized." 97% of these are in this Window.
...There are over 1.3 billion people living in the Window who have little or no chance to hear the gospel.
...In the Window, we find 86% of the people group which are less than 2% Christian.

...There are 500 people groups in the Window that have never heard the Gospel.

3) Christianity in the Window . . .

...Only 1.2% of all mission funds go to the Window.
...Only 1% of all Scripture distribution are distributed to the 10/40 Window.
...Only 3% of all the languages for which the Bible has been translated are directed toward the Window.
...9 out of the 10 countries where the physical persecution of Christians is the most severe are in the Window.
...The greatest revival ever on earth is taking place in the 10/40 Window countries of Asia. Every day in communist China over 25,000 people accept Christ. In India, an estimated 15,000 people are turning to Jesus daily. In the early eighties there were only 15,000 known Christians in the Himalayan country of Nepal compared to over 200,000 followers of Christ today.

One way to understand the severity of the problem concerning unreached people groups is to compare the number of people on the earth to the physical earth itself. By virtue of the rotation of the globe, roughly half of the world is without the light of the sun at any given time of the day, or what we might call 'in the dark.' So it is with the people of the world: just under half of the world's population is yet without the light of the glorious gospel. One missions writer points out the following facts: ".....of those 24,000 people groups (in the world), 14,000 of them already have a church that is unique to their culture and language. That means that there are only about 10,000 left! The task is over half completed! However, the bad news is that what is left is the hardest areas to reach with the Gospel."[107] These statistics should both alarm and arouse us: alarm us because so many have not heard of Christ, and arouse into doing our part to ensure that the gospel message gets to these people as soon as possible.

Knowing these facts, how is it that so many are still unmoved and unconcerned about evangelizing the lost? Christians are without excuse for their lack of effort to reach the masses yet in spiritual darkness. This is not the message of an overzealous religious enthusiast, but reflects the very heartbeat of God; evangelizing the lost. For this reason, missions should be the greatest concern of God's people.

Jesus Himself commissioned the Church to take the gospel to every nation (Mark 16:15; Acts 1:8). Paul as well showed his passion for the unreached when he wrote *"Yea, so have I strived to preach the gospel, not where Christ was named, lest I should build upon another man's foundation:"* (Romans 15:20) Charles Spurgeon wrote with enthusiasm: "Paul had an aggressive policy, he pushed into the enemy's territory, as all God's servants should endeavor to do, for multitudes are still ignorant of the name of Jesus."[108]

It was Robert Moffat (1795–1883), fellow missionary helper of David Livingstone who passionately stated: "I have seen, at different times, the smoke of a thousand villages–villages whose people are without Christ, without God, and without hope in this world."[109] May we as believers likewise open our eyes to the desperate need of the heathen who have yet to hear of Christ, so that we may endeavor to reach them with the gospel before they eternally perish.

101 The Eternal Worth of the Soul; A.W. Tozer
102 Life and Liberty Ministries, Missionary Quotes
103 Ibid
104 Let's Quit Kidding Ourselves About Missions, Moody Press. 1979;
105 James S. Huggins: www.jamesshuggins.com
106 http://1040window.org/
107 www.pasadenachristian.com/
108 Power BibleCD; Spurgeon's Devotional Notes.
109 BIMI Magazine, James Ray (editor), vol.2, 2006

Chapter Nine

~

The Workers

"...the laborers are few..." - Jesus

When studying this subject seriously, one soon realizes that the work of World Missions is a daunting task. Many souls remain unreached with the good news of the gospel, which leads to the next great challenge in missions: the need for Christian Workers. The work of the Master is of the utmost importance, yet there seems to be a severe shortage of willing workers. Unfortunately, many regard the work of missions as trivial and demeaning. An increasing number of Christian young people aspire to become successful in the modern world. There is nothing wrong with doing one's best in whatever life calling God has designed for an individual. However, for numerous reasons, far too many chase after fame and fortune without even considering God's perfect will for their life.

God is calling for His people to enter the harvest field to work for Him, but many forfeit the call in exchange for such things as possessions, power, and position in this world. These things obviously appear more glamorous and beneficial to their immediate circumstances, but will prove to be disappointing and disparaging in view of their eternity.

The true Christian Church needs a fresh outlook on the work of God in order to encourage individuals in the Church to give their lives to serving God and their fellow man. The following illustration helps us understand this point: "One of the large oil companies needed a public relations office for their work in the Orient. They asked a missionary to take over the post, offering a salary that was considerably larger than that which the church was able to pay, but he turned it down. The company officials met, and because they felt this missionary had unusual gifts in the field of public relations, they increased the salary offer to a point where it would be very difficult to say, 'No.' But again the missionary refused. 'What is wrong?' the official asked.

'Is not the salary big enough?' The reply was simple, yet direct: 'The salary is big enough, but the job is not.'"

In order to recruit workers for God's harvest, it is necessary to identify both the problem and the solution. All are likely to agree that Satan is the arch enemy of God and His saints. The devil is busy attempting to destroy God's work in this world, though he cannot force anyone to serve him or cause anyone to stop serving God. Satan is the master of deception and temptation, however, and some of the chief weapons he uses against the Church are discouragement, delight of sin, and distraction, all of which can be summarized in the term worldliness!

It is worthwhile to take notice of the warning of Paul as he challenged the Roman Christians to serve God with complete commitment as living sacrifices for Christ: *"And be not conformed to this world: but be ye transformed by the renewing of your mind, that ye may prove what is that good, and acceptable, and perfect, will of God."* (Romans 12:2) Albert Barnes makes these comments: "Christians should not conform to the maxims, habits, feelings, etc., of a wicked, luxurious, and idolatrous age, but should be conformed solely to the precepts and laws of the gospel; or the same principle may be extended to every age, and the direction may be, that Christians should not conform to the prevailing habits, style, and manners of the world--the people who know not God. They are to be governed by the laws of the Bible; to fashion their lives after the example of Christ; and to form themselves by principles different from those which prevail in the world."110

The world has no desire for the eternal things of God; to them this current world is all that matters. When Christians allow the cares and pleasures of this life to dominate their thinking and behavior, it can be truthfully said that they are becoming "worldly." A Christian may appear modest in appearance and denounce *rock and roll* or *country* music, but if they have no interest in reaching lost souls for Christ, they are still demonstrating a worldly spirit.

In his exceptional book *Why Men Go Back*, Charles W. Conn explains worldliness in this way: "Worldliness in short is living as if this world were the only one in which we will ever live. Anyone with a carnal mind, therefore, delights in and craves the pleasure, position, prosperity, prestige of this world. Anyone who is more taken up with the things of this world than the world to come is a worldly man!"111 This explanation begs the following questions: Are not men's souls eternal matters? How then can professing Christians place earthly matters ahead of eternal souls?

Following is a list of some of the fruits of a worldly spirit, viewed in the context of World Missions. Other problem areas could certainly be cited as well, but I believe these to be among the major evils confronting Christians today:

ONE: Apathy

The Old Testament Jewish prophet, Jeremiah, lived in a troubled time for his people Israel. God's covenant people were backslidden, and had begun to live as the heathen nations around them. Jeremiah describes the current situation by writing: *"For my people have committed two evils; they have forsaken me the fountain of living waters, and hewed them out cisterns, broken cisterns, that can hold no water."* (Jeremiah 2:13) Adam Clarke comments: "First, they forsook God, the Fountain of life, light, prosperity, and happiness. Secondly, they hewed out broken cisterns; they joined themselves to idols, from whom they could receive neither temporal nor spiritual good! Their conduct was the excess of folly and blindness. What we call here broken cisterns, means more properly such vessels as were ill made, not staunch, ill put together, so that the water leaked through them."112

The love of idols and pleasure took God's own people away from serving the true and living God. Sadly, "idolatry" and pleasure seeking are prevalent in today's church world as well. The rise of hedonism and materialism has without doubt distracted many professing Christians from their true purpose in life. In the words of one Christian leader, our life purpose as Christians should be: "To Know Christ and to Make Him Known!" The love of this present world causes people to be apathetic and indifferent to the things that matter most. This love for the world was a major problem of a city that came to be known as one of the most evil and vile of all cities, Sodom. The prophet Ezekiel noted: *"Behold, this was the iniquity of thy sister Sodom, pride, fullness of bread, and abundance of idleness was in her and in her daughters, neither did she strengthen the hand of the poor and needy."* (Ezekiel 16:49) Clarke wrote: "If we are to take this place literally, Sodom was guilty of other crimes besides that for which she appears to have been especially punished; in addition to her unnatural crime, She is charged with pride, luxury, idleness, and non-charitableness; and these were sufficient to sink any city to the bottomless pit."113

Pride of the heart will certainly lead to a cold and indifferent attitude toward others in need. All Christians must carefully guard against such ill conditions of heart and mind.

This problem of apathy and its effects on a life is illustrated by the Holy Spirit's record of the distressing account of Paul's former fellow laborer, Demas: *"For Demas hath forsaken me, having loved this present world, and is departed unto Thessalonica; Crescens to Galatia, Titus unto Dalmatia."* (2 Timothy 4:10) Demas left the work of God because of his love for the world. We are not told specifically what Demas did with the rest of his life, but we can surmise that he sought a life of comfort and ease instead of paying the price to serve God.

Apathy is a subtle and dangerous condition of the heart. It is easy to lose the burden for others and for the things of God. Jeremiah was alarmed that no one seemed to care about the spiritual condition of God's covenant people. He wrote "Is *it nothing to you, all ye that pass by? behold, and see if there be any sorrow like unto my sorrow, which is done unto me, wherewith the LORD hath afflicted me in the day of his fierce anger."* (Lamentations 1:12)

There is no excuse for the existence of indifference in the Christian Church. The fact that Jesus Christ gave His life so that mankind could be graciously saved from sin's punishment and have everlasting life should be enough to motivate Christians to reach others with the same *Good News* that saved them.

The chief motivation for evangelizing the lost should be *love!* Paul wrote, *"For the love of Christ constraineth us; because we thus judge, that if one died for all, then were all dead: And that he died for all, that they which live should not henceforth live unto themselves, but unto him which died for them, and rose again."* (2 Corinthians 5:14-15) This verse reveals the heart of the problem of those who refuse to labor for Christ to reach others with the gospel: their love for Christ is lacking!

The love of self makes one apathetic toward others, but a genuine love for Christ results in true appreciation for His will and a desire to do it. God's Word reveals that His will is for mankind to hear the message of salvation and be saved before they perish. It has been observed that: "Love will find a way - indifference will find an excuse."[114]

When we look at some of the statistics regarding the church in America, one has to wonder if Christians have lost much of their zeal for Christ and His work. Consider the following report by the Barna Research Group:

- 49% of born again Christians shared their faith in Christ in the past year taking a non-Christian friend to church so they could hear the gospel. (2004)
- 78% of born again Christians shared their faith in Christ within the past year by offering to pray with a non-Christian person who was in need of encouragement or support. (2004)
- 21% of born again people shared their faith in Christ with a non-Christian person in the past year by sending letters or e-mails explaining aspects of their faith and encouraging them to consider it more closely. (2004)
- The majority of born again Christians (59%) feel a sense of responsibility to share their faith. (2006) [115]

Though these statistics might not seem all that terrible, consider that only a little more than half of professing Christians have a conviction about sharing their faith. This means that almost half of the Christians in America feel no obligation to share the message of eternal hope with the lost here in their homeland, much less in a foreign land about which they most likely know very little.

Apathy toward the mandate to reach the world for Christ is obviously still a problem in the Church, and it is evident that we need a revival of passion for the lost. This hymn by Herbert Tovey demonstrates the attitude we should have:

Give me a passion for souls, dear Lord, A passion to save the lost; O that Thy love were by all adored, And welcomed at any cost.

Refrain: *Jesus, I long, I long to be winning Men who are lost, and constantly sinning; O may this hour be one of beginning The story of pardon to tell.*

Though there are dangers untold and stern Confronting me in the way, Willingly still would I go, nor turn, But trust Thee for grace each day.

How shall this passion for souls be mine? Lord, make Thou the answer clear; Help me to throw out the old life line, To those who are struggling near.

TWO: Affluence

Closely related to *apathy*, another reason for an indifferent spirit is *affluence*. The dictionary defines affluence as: "1) a: an abundant flow or supply: PROFUSION b: abundance of property: WEALTH; 2) a flowing to or toward a point : INFLUX" 116

It is important to remember that it is not sinful to have things. However, when the desire to obtain and possess worldly goods drives and controls us, it becomes immoral and destructive. Paul referred to this when he explained to believers of his day: *"But godliness with contentment is great gain. For we brought nothing into this world, and it is certain we can carry nothing out. And having food and raiment let us be therewith content. But they that will be rich fall into temptation and a snare, and into many foolish and hurtful lusts, which drown men in destruction and perdition. For the love of money is the root of all evil: which while some coveted after, they have erred from the*

faith, and pierced themselves through with many sorrows.”
(1 Timothy 6:6-10)

Notice that Paul does not say that money or possessions are inherently evil, only the love of them. Matthew Poole, the eminent Bible commentator, gives his insight on these words of Paul by writing: “…money itself is not evil, but the immoderate love of it, whether discerned in an over eager desire after it, or an excessive delight in it, is the cause of much evil, both of sin and punishment.”117

Excessive desire for the things of this world will not only harm the one who possesses it, but will end up hurting others as well, either directly or indirectly. The following exposition of 1Timothy 6:10 further explains this concept.

I. The Lust for Affluence (vs. 10).

Most of us desire money and things to some extent. Money, or in some societies other forms of capital, is needed to pay for the necessities of life. The Lord acknowledged this when He commanded Adam to work for his bread. Paul also taught this fact of life when he wrote *“Let him that stole steal no more: but rather let him labor, working with his hands the thing which is good, that he may have to give to him that needeth.”* (Ephesians 4:28)

The real issue that we must guard against is an excessive love or lust for money and affluence. Christians must maintain a proper perspective concerning these things. When the desire for possessions becomes an all-consuming drive, it is both sinful and destructive. God's Word admonishes us to *“flee these things and follow after righteousness, godliness, faith, love, patience, meekness”* (v. 11).

II. The Lie of Affluence (vs. 10).

It is the main objective of Satan to deceive people everywhere, including Christians. One tool he uses to accomplish this goal is the love of money and affluence. He endeavors to tempt Christians to love their money and possessions more than they love God. However, prayer, perseverance, and the promises of God's Word can enable Christians to resist the devil. Loving God completely and giving Him first place in their affections will provide believers a constant safeguard from such deception. The Scripture urges *"Fight the good fight of faith, lay hold on eternal life."*

III. The Loss through Affluence (vs. 10)

Countless souls have been destroyed by the lust of money and affluence. Men have lied, stolen, cheated, and even murdered for money. Possessions in almost any form can be a blessing. Affluence can bring glory to God if used correctly and unselfishly. However, the wrong use of money can bring destruction of body, mind, and soul. The Scripture says, *"But they that will be rich fall into temptation and a snare, and into many foolish and hurtful lusts, which drown men in destruction and perdition"* (v. 9). The remedy to such loss and destruction is found in the words of Jesus who admonished His followers to *"...seek ye first the kingdom of God, and his righteousness; and all these things shall be added unto you"* (Matthew 6:33).

A greater loss than a Christian falling away from the faith due to covetousness is that this person, called to be a witness for Christ (Acts 1:8), will cease to fulfill his vital mission. Jesus told His followers to be "lights" of the world (Matthew 5:14), but when materialism and affluence dominate the believer, it aids in extinguishing the spiritual flame of a passion for souls!

Unquestionably, God would have all of His saints to demonstrate the same spirit that is witnessed in the following true story: "A young man accepted for the African missionary field reported at New York for 'passage,' but found on further examination that his wife could not stand the climate. He was heartbroken, but he prayerfully returned to his home and determined to make all the money he could to be used in spreading the Kingdom of God over the world. His father, a dentist, had started to make, on the side, an unfermented wine for the communion service. The young man took the business over and developed it until it assumed vast proportions—his name was 'Charles E. Welch,' whose family still manufactures grape juice. He has given literally hundreds of thousands of dollars to the work of missions."[118]

The remarkable reality concerning this matter of affluence is that material wealth cannot and never will make any one truly happy. Peace and joy only come when we take what God has provided for us and use it to be a blessing to others for Him and His glory. This fact is clearly expressed in the following quote from the theologian Augustine: "Where your pleasure is, there is your treasure; where your treasure is, there is your heart; where your heart is, there is your happiness."[119]

THREE: Attrition and Apprehension

The final point I wish to discuss in this section concerns *Attrition* and *Apprehension*. These issues provide another major reason why so many Christians do not become involved in World Missions.

Attrition:

Attrition refers to withdrawing or turning from the work someone was once a part of. As mentioned earlier, Demas fits this description - (2 Timothy 4:10).

The following is a recent report concerning the attrition rates in modern missions:

"During a 3-year period studied (2002-2005 AD), about 4,400 missionaries from participating agencies left the field (for all reasons) without intentions of returning.

Generalization: about 6.4% of the total missionary force leaves the field every year for all reasons (7.75 % when statistically adjusted to reflect fast growing agencies)."[120]

Following are the top reasons given for Christian workers choosing to leave the mission field:

"The main reason for missionaries leaving the field vary by country. In the Old Sending countries (Australia, Denmark, Germany, UK, Canada and USA) the top five reasons were normal retirement (11%), child(ren) (11%), a change of job (9%), health problems (9%), and problems with peer missionaries on the field (6%).

In the New Sending countries (Brazil, Costa Rica, Ghana, Nigeria, India, Korea, Philippines, Singapore) the top 5 were lack of home support (8%), lack of clear call (8%), inadequate commitment (7%), disagreements with the sending agency (6%), and problems with peer missionaries (6%)."[121]

These are disappointing statistics, especially considering the shortage already of laborers on the mission field. The Church must continue to investigate this problem and do whatever is necessary to prevent it from continuing. There will always be what missiologists refer to as *acceptable attrition*, which includes retirement, sickness, and issues related to children. However, the attrition that is most problematic is that which is called *Preventable Attrition* because of lack of home support (not just financial), problems with personal concerns, lack of call (dealt with before field service), inadequate pre-field training, poor cultural adaptation, and a few other reasons.

In his book entitled *Too Valuable to Lose*, Dr. William D. Taylor has offered the following areas that must be addressed in order to prevent missionary attrition:

"The first is the pre-candidate component: the mobilization of the church and the selection of the missionary, including screening, sending, and supporting.

The second is the training component: the effective equipping of the cross-cultural force.

The third is the field component: supporting, strategizing, shepherding, and supervising the global missionary force."[122]

It would be unwise and heartless of me or anyone else to say that it is always wrong for a person(s) to leave the mission field for any reason other than an acceptable one. There is what missions experts call *Desirable but Unrealized Attrition:* when missionaries who should leave remain on the field, compounding problems in that their presence forces some of the better missionaries to go elsewhere. However, the fact remains that the Church still must seek to help prevent missionary attrition from happening on a regular and growing basis. Statistics show some degree of neglect in this extremely important area of Church responsibility. It should come as no surprise then that World Missions leader Steve Richardson reports: "Recent research in the area of missionary attrition confirms that 'a low sense of organizational connectedness' is one of the most important factors contributing to the early departure of missionaries."123

At the risk of sounding overly simplistic, the obvious suggestion in answer to these challenges in missions is prayer, as well as a willingness to work together as a team. Our guidebook is the Bible, but to be effective, biblical principles and mandates must be put into practice. Foreign Missionaries and other Christian workers need to see their role as just one part in the whole of God's harvest field. In essence, we are soldiers in the same army, players on the same team; so then we must work together to see the Kingdom of God advanced. The following story illustrates this point well: "In May, 1953, two men became the first in history to climb to the top of Mt. Everest; Edmund Hillary, a New Zealand beekeeper and explorer, and his Sherpa guide from Nepal, Tenzing Norgay. They reached the summit together and attained instant international fame.

On the way down from the 29,000-foot peak, Hillary slipped and started to fall. He would almost certainly have fallen to his death, but Tenzing Norgay immediately dug in his ice-axe and braced the rope linking them together, saving Hillary's life.

At the bottom the International Press made a huge fuss over the Sherpa guide's heroic action. Through it all, Tenzing Norgay remained very calm, professional, and non-carried away by it all. To all the shouted questions he had one simple answer: 'Mountain climbers always help each other.' "124

Apprehension:

Apprehension is the role that fear and doubt play in causing some Christians to hold back from getting involved in missions work. Though many years have passed since the days of the first disciples of Christ, many of the same problems and difficulties that they faced still exist among Christians of today. They were given a mandate to be witnesses for Christ, yet we see that they had challenges 'getting off of the launch pad.'

On one occasion we read: *"Then the same day at evening, being the first day of the week, when the doors were shut where the disciples were assembled for fear of the Jews, came Jesus and stood in the midst, and saith unto them, Peace be unto you."* (John 20:19). Doubt and fear dominated the minds of Christ's potential 'fishers of men.' Similarly, many Christians today are living in anxiety over things that they have absolutely no control over. I can appreciate the following quote simply because it is so true: "The man who fears suffering is already suffering from what he fears."[125]

When Jesus told the Church to go and fulfill the Great Commission, it was understood that He would constantly be with them. Far too many followers of Christ have not believed His promises. God promises the following in His Word:

Joshua 1:5 "There shall not any man be able to stand before thee all the days of thy life: as I was with Moses, so I will be with thee: I will not fail thee, nor forsake thee."
Isaiah 41:10 "Fear thou not; for I am with thee: be not dismayed; for I am thy God: I will strengthen thee; yea, I will help thee; yea, I will uphold thee with the right hand of my righteousness."
Matthew 28:20 "...lo, I am with you alway, even unto the end of the world. Amen".

Related to this verse (Matthew 28:20) is the following excerpt from the journal of the great missionary explorer David Livingstone:

"January 14, 1856. Evening. 'Felt much turmoil of spirit in prospect of having all my plans for the welfare of this great region and this teeming population knocked on the head by savages to-morrow. But I read that Jesus said: 'All power is given unto Me in heaven and in earth. Go ye therefore, and teach all nations, and lo, I am with you alway, even unto the end of the world.' It is the word of a gentleman of the most strict and sacred honour, so there's an end of it! I will not cross furtively to-night as I intended. Should such a man as I flee? Nay, verily, I shall take observations for latitude and longitude to-night, though they may be the last. I feel quite calm now, thank God!'"126

When a follower of Christ is tempted to 'play it safe' and risk little or nothing to promote the cause of Christ, it is an insult to the One who gave all He had to save lost humanity. We must, of course, use wisdom in all we do and should strive to live safe, lengthy and healthy lives as best we know how. However, when it comes to the call of God to reach others for Christ, His servants must be willing to say "*yes*" even at the risk of life and safety. This was the attitude of the song writer C. Austin Miles who wrote:

It may be I must carry,
The blessed word of life
Across the burning deserts
To those in sinful strife.
And though it may be my lot
To bear my colours there;
If Jesus goes with me, I'll go anywhere!

Fear, doubt, and apprehension are all the work of the flesh and the devil, which are both resistant to the will of God. The wise man said, *"He that observeth the wind shall not sow; and he that regardeth the clouds shall not reap."* (Ecclesiastes 11:4) In our human perspective of life, there will never be 'perfect' circumstances fully conducive to the work of missions. There will always be enemies and obstacles attempting to hinder the plan of God. However, with Christ by our side, believers can take bold steps to proclaim the good news to lost souls everywhere, in spite of the 'winds of adversity.' I find this small portion of

Livingstone's biography written by F.W. Boreham to be challenging and inspiring:

"Later in the same year (1856), he pays his first visit to the homeland. Honors are everywhere heaped upon him. The University of Glasgow confers upon him the degree of Doctor of Laws. On such occasions the recipient of the honor is usually subjected to some banter at the hands of the students. But when Livingstone rises, bearing upon his person the marks of his struggles and sufferings in darkest Africa, he is received in reverential silence. He is gaunt and haggard as a result of his long exposure to the tropical sun. On nearly thirty occasions he has been laid low by the fevers that steam from the inland swamps, and these severe illnesses have left their mark. His left arm, crushed by the lion, hangs helplessly at his side. A hush falls upon the great assembly as he announces his resolve to return to the land for which he has already endured so much. 'But I return,' he says, 'without misgiving and with great gladness. For would you like me to tell you what supported me through all the years of exile among people whose language I could not understand, and whose attitude towards me was always uncertain and often hostile? It was this: *Lo, I am with you alway, even unto the end of the world!" On those words I staked everything, and they never failed!'"[127]

Not only do Christians at times fear dangerous situations and undesirable circumstances, they may also fear entering God's work because of a sense of inadequacy.

God knows exactly what He is doing when He puts His hand upon someone, choosing that person for service. Many have felt that perhaps God was calling them to serve Him in some specific way, as a missionary, a pastor, or some other calling. They may hesitate because they assume that God just could not use them. They convince themselves that they are too young, or too old, or perhaps they feel that they do not have enough talent, or that they are not outgoing enough.

When the Lord pricks a person's heart during a missions conference, they may respond by telling God that He has the wrong person. Reasoning like this causes people to miss out on God's best for their lives. Some Christians have no doubt been burdened to get involved in soul winning, but are convinced that they do not have what it takes to be involved with that particular ministry. Perhaps there are some who should be teaching Sunday School, but remain sidelined because they do not believe that they can be used by God.

It was this sense of inadequacy that caused Moses to offer a lame complaint when God called him to lead the people of Israel out of captivity. In essence, he was saying to God "You have the wrong person!" Exodus 3:11-12 states: *"And Moses said unto God, Who am I, that I should go unto Pharaoh, and that I should bring forth the children of Israel out of Egypt? And he said, Certainly I will be with thee; and this shall be a token unto thee, that I have sent thee: When thou hast brought forth the people out of Egypt, ye shall serve God upon this mountain."*

There are many reasons why Moses should not have been apprehensive to fulfill the mission he was assigned to by the one and only Jehovah. A few of these reasons are:

1) Moses was one of God's chosen vessels. The Lord also said this to Saul of Tarsus after he received salvation on the Damascus Road. *"But the Lord said unto him, Go thy way: for he is a chosen vessel unto me, to bear my name before the Gentiles, and kings, and the children of Israel:"* (Acts 9:15) In essence, all Christians who have experienced true salvation are chosen vessels to work for Christ. Believers should recognize that God made them who they are. In 1 Corinthians 15:10 we read: *"But by the grace of God I am what I am: and his grace which was bestowed upon me was not in vain; but I laboured more abundantly than they all: yet not I, but the grace of God which was with me."*

2) God has promised to be with His chosen vessel. God told Moses in Exodus 3:12 *"And he said, Certainly I will be with thee;..."* This same promise was also given to Joshua, Moses' successor: *"There shall not any man be able to stand before thee all the days of thy life: as I was with Moses, so I will be with thee: I will not fail thee, nor forsake thee."* (Joshua 1:5)

3) God Himself sent Moses, for we read in verse 10: "*Come now therefore, and I will send thee unto Pharaoh, that thou mayest bring forth my people the children of Israel out of Egypt.*" In a similar way, Christ has sent all Christians to help deliver souls held captive in sin. Matthew 28:19-20 tells us, "*Go ye therefore, and teach all nations, baptizing them in the name of the Father, and of the Son, and of the Holy Ghost: Teaching them to observe all things whatsoever I have commanded you: and, lo, I am with you alway, even unto the end of the world. Amen.*"

4) The God that sends is the great I AM! Exodus 3:13-15 reads as follows: "*And Moses said unto God, Behold, when I come unto the children of Israel, and shall say unto them, The God of your fathers hath sent me unto you; and they shall say to me, What is his name? what shall I say unto them? And God said unto Moses, I AM THAT I AM: and he said, Thus shalt thou say unto the children of Israel, I AM hath sent me unto you. And God said moreover unto Moses, Thus shalt thou say unto the children of Israel, The LORD God of your fathers, the God of Abraham, the God of Isaac, and the God of Jacob, hath sent me unto you: this is my name for ever, and this is my memorial unto all generations.*"

As God assured Moses, He wants to convince each of us that He is the all-powerful God who has all things in His control. Paul reminded the Roman Christians: "*.....If God be for us, who can be against us?*" (Romans 8:31) Church history provides us many examples of saints who were fearless in the face of opposition and never retreated from fulfilling God's will in reaching the world for Christ. Following is one such account: "Seeking to know God better, John Chrysostom became a hermit in the mountains near Antioch in A.D. 373. Although his time of isolation was cut short by illness, he learned that with God at his side, he could stand alone against anyone or anything. That lesson served Chrysostom well. In A.D. 398 he was appointed patriarch of Constantinople, where his zeal for reform antagonized the Empress Eudoxi, who had him exiled. Allowed to return after a short time, Chrysostom again infuriated Eudoxia, who sent him away again. How did

Chrysostom respond to such persecution? With these words: "What can I fear? Will it be death? But you know that Christ is my life, and that I shall gain by death. Will it be exile? But the earth and all its fullness are the Lord's. Poverty I do not fear; riches I do not sigh for; and from death I do not shrink." 128

This sacrificial attitude is reflected in the seal and motto of one particular Missions organization. It is reported that "'Ready for Either' is the significant legend that under spans the seal of the Baptist Missionary Union, which presents an ox standing with a plough on one side, and an altar on the other."

At times we may feel that we are not making much of a difference in the realm of world missions, so we tend to stay less involved, or quit altogether. This is the design of the devil! God views success differently than man. To God, success means faithfulness to the calling He has placed on one's life. God is simply looking for a heart totally surrendered to His will and work.

Not everyone can emulate the Apostle Paul, Amy Carmichael, or David Livingstone who outwardly achieved much for God's kingdom, but all can be faithful to their individual calling. If we allow fear and doubt to keep us from following God's will in the direction that He leads us, there will be some who eternally suffer as a result of our disobedience. Our willingness to heed God's call, no matter what it is He asks of us, will be sure to make a difference.

The following true story should convince us that the little we may do can have a definite impact on our world for Christ; "Sir Michael Costa was conducting a rehearsal in which the orchestra was joined by a great chorus. About halfway through the session, with trumpets blaring, drums rolling, and violins singing their rich melody, the piccolo player muttered to himself, 'What good am I doing? I might as well not be playing. Nobody can hear me anyway.' So he placed his instrument to his lips but made no sound. Within moments the conductor cried, 'Stop! Stop! Where's the piccolo?' Perhaps many people did not realize that the piccolo was missing, but the most important one did. So it is in the Christian life. God knows when we do not play the part assigned to us, even if others do not."129

Lastly, I desire to discuss an important issue which causes apprehension in some about reaching others around the world with the gospel of Jesus Christ. It is a fear that most people do not like to admit: a phobia of other kinds of people and cultures different from their own. In a word, it is *prejudice*, often surfacing because of certain preconceived ideas held.

Prejudice is very much like the disease of cancer: it is aggressive and damaging, with far reaching effects. Prejudice destroys lives and relationships and hinders our ability to function as we were designed and intended to. There are few remedies in medicine that would be as welcomed as the cure for cancer. So it is in the spiritual world: when one is delivered from any work of the flesh, the result is a liberty which causes great rejoicing.

Apprehension concerning reaching out to others of a different nationality or culture is a terrible bondage that must be broken if we are to be of any use to God in His harvest field. In missiological terms, this fear is referred to as *Xenophobia*: a phobic attitude toward strangers or the unknown. The Greek words ξένος (xenos), meaning "foreigner," "stranger," and φόβος (phobos), meaning "fear." The term is typically used to describe fear or dislike of foreigners or in general people different from one's self. This fear does not have to do with differences of one's skin or hair color as much as it does with differences of culture and language.

In his autobiography, Mahatma Gandhi wrote that during his student days he read the Gospels seriously and considered converting to Christianity. One Christian devotional said, "He believed that in the teachings of Jesus he could find the solution to the caste system that was dividing the people of India. So one Sunday he decided to attend services at a nearby church and talk to the minister about becoming a Christian. When he entered the sanctuary, however, the usher refused to give him a seat and suggested that he go worship with his own people. Gandhi left the church and never returned. 'If Christians have caste differences also,' he said, 'I might as well remain a Hindu.'"130 Sadly, the usher's prejudice and discrimination not only betrayed Jesus but turned an eternal soul away from trusting Him as Savior.

Christian author Dr. Neil Rendall gives this needed insight on the problem of prejudice: "We are a people in the process of change. But change, any change, threatens most of us. This is part of the tension we feel as we look at the world and nation in which we live. When the changes involve people groups of different ethnic origins, the tensions and fears can be even more intense and more confusing."131 I appreciate the honesty and accuracy of Dr. Rendall's statement.

If the Church is to be effective, it must deal with its faults and ask the Lord to correct them. Regrettably, there are likely born-again believers who are still in denial of possessing some form of Xenophobia. The first step to overcoming such fears is to acknowledge the problem, for only then can we find the solution. Any Christian having difficulty in this area of phobia or prejudice toward a different people group or culture can rest assured that they are not alone. Luke provides us with a story germane to this topic involving the Apostle Peter and his struggle to accept certain Gentiles into the Church. This account is found in the book of Acts, chapters 10 and 11.

Acts chapter 10 is about two visions, one by the Apostle Simon Peter in Joppa and the other by Cornelius a Roman Centurion in Caesarea. In the first vision, God prepared Peter's heart to accept Gentiles, whom he had before rejected, as equal under the grace of God. In the end, Peter was obedient to the truth and reversed his prejudiced thinking. We find record of this change in Acts chapter 11 where he recounts his experience with other Apostles and Messianic Christians. Paul later wrote and concluded in Galatians 3:8 *"(In Christ) There is neither Jew nor Greek, slave nor free, male nor female."*

Not everyone with Xenophobia or other forms of bigotry holds the degree of prejudice that Peter had. However, all Christians can learn from Peter's story and find help for their shortcomings, just as Peter did from his experience.

In order for any cure to work, it must be administered just as the physician prescribes. Like a doctor, God provided Peter with a cure for his apprehension of ministering to the Gentiles. The Lord's treatment is threefold:

1). God wanted Peter to recognize the Depth of His prejudice.

In Acts 10:14, Peter tells the Lord, *"...Not so, Lord; for I have never eaten any thing that is common or unclean."* Peter was well aware of his past and acknowledged it honestly. Jonah had a problem comparable to Peter's with a people that were not of the same country, religion, and culture as himself. Jonah's attitude toward the Ninevites was certainly not one of compassion or eternal concern. The disciples of Jesus displayed a similar attitude toward the Syro-Phoenecian woman of whom we read: *"Then Jesus went...into the coasts of Tyre and Sidon. And, behold, a woman of Canaan came out of the same coasts, and cried unto him, saying, Have mercy on me, O Lord, thou Son of David; my daughter is grievously vexed with a devil. But he answered her not a word. And his disciples came and besought him, saying, Send her away; for she crieth after us."* (Matthew 15:21-23)

At times, prejudice and bigotry is not only directed at those who are of a different religion, gender, nationality or ethnic background, but also toward those of a different socio-economic status, or whose lifestyle does not measure up to our own high moral standard. As Bible believing Christians, we must point out the wrong in any people group and should not tolerate sin, either in ourselves or any other individual from our homeland or a foreign land. However, we must treat people as Jesus did, with dignity and respect, not despising them because they are of a different nationality, religion, or social class.

Jesus understood that every soul is made in the image of God and is redeemable by His own blood if they would but repent and believe upon Him. This includes radical Islamic terrorists, prostitutes, homosexuals and abortionists. We cannot accept their lifestyles and should continue to vehemently despise their behavior; but must at the same time pray for them and ask God to make the gospel message available to them.

The following account should inspire every forgiven Christian to do more to win the enemies of Christ with the gospel:

"Stephen Olford tells of a Baptist pastor during the American Revolution, Peter Miller, who lived in Ephrata, Pennsylvania, and enjoyed the friendship of George Washington. In Ephrata also lived Michael Wittman, an evil-minded sort who did all he could to oppose and humiliate the pastor. One day Michael Wittman was arrested for treason and sentenced to die. Peter Miller traveled seventy miles on foot to Philadelphia to plead for the life of the traitor. "No, Peter," General Washington said. "I cannot grant you the life of your friend." "My friend!" exclaimed the old preacher. "He's the bitterest enemy I have." "What?" cried Washington. "You have walked seventy miles to save the life of an enemy? That puts the matter in different light. I will grant your pardon." And he did. Peter Miller took Michael Wittman back home to Ephrata--no longer an enemy but a friend."[132]

Who can forget the remarkable story of Elisabeth Elliot, wife of Jim Elliot, the missionary who was martyred with four of his missionary co-workers by the Aucas Indians in South America. She, along with their baby, Valerie, went back to these same Indians and began sharing the gospel with them. Through remarkable providence, Elisabeth met two Auca women who came to live with her for one year. These women were the key which opened up the opportunity for Elisabeth to go in and live with the same tribe that had killed her own husband and the four other missionaries. She remained there for two years and won many of those souls to the Lord. Only God could give a person such a forgiving and compassionate spirit!

2). God wanted Peter to have a Desire to change.

In Acts 10:6 we find that Peter is staying with Simon the tanner, who works with the hides of dead animals. Leviticus 11 made clear to the Jews what animals are to be considered clean and unclean. The law also clearly stated that even touching the carcass of one of these animals unknowingly would make one unclean. Scripture does not tell us that this particular tanner only dealt in hides that were considered clean. As well, many of the carcasses were only considered defiled until evening. Either way, it is obvious that Peter was willing to take the risk of staying with a tanner. While he may not have eaten of the unclean thing, it did not disturb him to be around it. It is possible that God was preparing Peter's heart to have his intolerance of others changed. While it is true that Christians must not tolerate any form of sin, some are intolerant not because of sin, but rather because they simply do not care for the ways of others.

Too often, Christians separate over issues that have nothing to do with Biblical principles of righteousness. Those who are unwilling to accept truly born again Christians who are not unrighteous or worldly according to the Bible, commit sin.

James explained this idea when he wrote: *"My brethren, have not the faith of our Lord Jesus Christ, the Lord of glory, with respect of persons. For if there come unto your assembly a man with a gold ring, in goodly apparel, and there come in also a poor man in vile raiment; And ye have respect to him that weareth the gay clothing, and say unto him, Sit thou here in a good place; and say to the poor, Stand thou there, or sit here under my footstool: Are ye not then partial in yourselves, and are become judges of evil thoughts?"* (James 2:1-4)

If believers cannot be unified with genuine Christians of their own nationality and culture, it is certain that they will not have a desire to win those of a different ethnic group, simply because they are afraid of their differences.

3). God wanted Peter to embrace a Duty to love all (v. 15)

God's love is not the same as the world's love. John said *"God is love."* Love is His very nature. God has what we call *agape* love; unconditional in the sense that no one can earn God's favor or acceptance on their own. God's love looks beyond sin and defilement of soul. However, God's love alone cannot save a person, for there must be a price paid for sin. God is not only love, for He is just and holy as well. God demands payment for man's sin, and that is where Jesus Christ's part of the plan of salvation comes in. John 3:16 says: *"For God so loved the world, that he gave his only begotten Son, that whosoever believeth in him should not perish, but have everlasting life."* The agape love of God is what made it possible for Jesus to forgive His enemies who nailed Him to the cross. It is that same love which forgave us, for it was while we were yet sinners that Christ died for us. (Romans 5:8)

Jesus' cruel death on the cross proves two important truths: first, God hates and will not tolerate sin; second, He loves all men so much that He gave His best to provide a way out so that they would not have to perish eternally. Jesus was God in human flesh, and by His very life showed mankind the heart of the Father. Jesus said in John 14:9 *"...he that hath seen me hath seen the Father."* Jesus went about doing good (Acts 10:38) and having compassion on people, regardless of nationality, social status or gender. Here are a few examples:

- Healing a leper by touching him (Matt 8)
- Healing a Centurion's servant (a gentile) (Matt 8)
- Calling a tax collector to be a disciple   (Matt 8)
- Healing a woman's' daughter (a gentile) (Matt 15)
- Healing two blind men by touch (Matt 20)
- Casting out a demon then taking the boy by the hand (Mark 9)
- Raises the son of a widow from the dead (touches the coffin) (Luke 7)
- Allowing a sinful woman to touch Him (lifestyle problem) (Luke 7)
- Healing 3 women (gender barrier) (Luke 8)
- Portraying the "good Samaritan" as a neighbor (ethnic barrier) (Luke 10)
- Samaritan leper is healed and gives thanks (ethnic barrier) (Luke 17)
- A visit to the house of Zacchaeus (Luke 19)
- The Samaritan woman at the well (ethnic and gender barriers) (John 4)
- The woman caught in adultery (John 8)

This matter begs the question, "What exactly is the cure for the cancer of prejudice and bigotry?" The answer can be summed up with the words of Christ to His followers, *"Thou shalt love thy neighbor as thyself.:"* Matthew 22:39 One commentator wrote the following about Jesus' command: "One who loves his neighbor as himself, will seek the welfare of those around him."[133] Our neighbor is the whole of humanity, to whom Christians are obligated to love and to give the gospel to. *"Let us not love in word only,"* states the Apostle John, *"but also in deed and truth."*

Sadly, some Christians have the attitude, 'If they are different from me, I cannot properly love or appreciate them.' As humans, we have the ability to formulate preconceived ideas about people that are not just like us. The following story helps us to understand this point: "William Pitt, former prime minister of England, once was conversing with one of his guests, when the latter suddenly offered him an apology. 'But we have just met,' Pitt remarked in surprise. 'That is just it sir,' said the visitor. 'I want to apologize for what I thought of you before we met each other.'"[134]

Jesus was able to show love and compassion without rejecting the person or accepting their sin. In every case He loved them unconditionally and charged them to not return to their sin. This is the model we should live by. One final story should help prove that God wants us to have a burden for all sinners, regardless of their nationality, culture, economic or social status. In doing so, we will not only make a difference in the individual lives which God leads us to, but we may potentially impact an entire nation for Christ!

Dr. Jonathan Bonk, Professor of Global Christian Studies at Providence Theological Seminary in Otterburne, Manitoba, has reminded us that: "God's way has always been to work through unimpressive peoples and gatherings, not through impressive shows of corporate and organizational strength."[135]

Bonk tells the story of how one of the greatest Christian movements in our century began in the Winnipeg YMCA, when John Hayward befriended Bakht Singh, then a young engineering student alone and far away from home in the autumn of 1929. Because Hayward practiced hospitality [Romans 12:13] -- in contrast to xenophobia, (dread of strangers), Singh became a believer and was discipled, returning to India in 1933 not as an agricultural engineer but as one of India's leading apostles in this century, responsible for establishing nearly 1,000 congregations around India, Pakistan, Sri Lanka and the USA. To his evangelistic ministry, furthermore, may be traced the ministries of many of the leading missionaries and ministries in India and Nepal. John Hayward did not profess a great desire for the masses, but he did show hospitality to a stranger at the YMCA. And his faithfulness to the simple biblical mandate allowed the Holy Spirit to do a mighty work."[136]

110 Power Bible CD; Barnes Notes on Romans 12:2.
111 Charles W. Conn; Why Men Go Back; (Pathway Press; Cleveland, TN; 1966; p. 58)
112 Power Bible CD; Clarke's notes on Jere. 2:13
113 Power Bible CD; Clarke's commentary on Ezekiel 16:49
114 Pulpit Helps
115 www.barna.org
116 Merriam-Webster Dictionary
117 Power Bible CD; Matthew Poole on 1 Tim. 6:10.
118 The Presbyterian Advance
119 http://www.sermonillustrations.com
120 Generating Change 2005
121 www.ywam.com
122 http://www.missionfrontiers.org
123 Steve Richardson. Director, PIONEERS-USA
124 E. M. Gershater, communications manager, Nationwide Insurance, Columbus, Ohio.
125 Instant Quotation Dictionary; Michel de Montaigne
126 www.wholesomewords.com; Biography of David Livingstone
127 www.wholesomewords.com; Biography of David Livingstone
128 Today in the Word, MBI, October, 1991, p. 33
129 http://www.tanbible.com
130 Our Daily Bread March 6, 1994.
131 Urbana Publications
132 The Grace of Giving: by Lynn Jost
133 PNTC, comments on Matthew 22:39
134 Elbourne Illustrations
135 (J. Kevin Livingston); sermon
136 (J. Kevin Livingston) International Ministries Consultation

Part Five
¥

Church History
and
World Missions

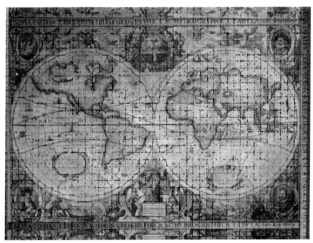

CHARLES PAHLMAN D. MIN.

When we consider the future of World Missions, it is helpful to have a proper understanding of the Church's past. Alphonse de Lamartine, French historian, promoted this principle when he wrote: "History teaches everything, even the future."

A careful examination of the lives of great Christians and leaders of the early Church, will help to educate and inspire our present generation to become more effective in our own attempt to reach the world for Christ in the same way.

Biographies from both the present and the past tell exciting experiences of some of the greatest missionaries who ever lived. Discovering the stories of Christians who have heard and obeyed God's call to be a cross-cultural witness can be a mind-opening and life-changing experience. Autobiographies and personal journals are especially encouraging as one hears directly from saints who have walked before us the road of service and sacrifice, often full of desires, doubts and questions.

Unfortunately, yet understandably, there will not be enough space in this book to highlight every Christian who has worked to expand the gospel message in their day. Following, however, are the stories of a few of the individuals who have been an inspiration to me, personally. I trust their testimonies and experiences will have a positive impact on the reader's desire to become more involved in World Missions.

The following biographies have been kept brief and are intended only to "whet the appetite" of you, the reader, and to encourage you to obtain a copy of their life story in order to read it in its entirety.

CHARLES PAHLMAN D. MIN.

Chapter Ten

~

In the Past

The majority of the following information was compiled and published by other authors, and is used here by their permission and blessing.

Patrick: (389-461AD)
Missionary to Ireland.

Patrick was born in Scotland. His father was a Roman centurion and also a deacon in a local New Testament church. Patrick was captured and taken to Ireland as a slave, but he escaped. After his conversion to Christ, he studied on the mainland in Gaul, and then returned to the heathen tribes in Ireland as a missionary. He began scores of churches and baptized--immersed--thousands of converts. He is largely responsible for the large number of Bible-believing Christians in Northern Ireland, Scotland, and England. Patrick, his father, and also his grandfather, were proud of the fact that they were not controlled by the Roman (Catholic) Church, and that they were responsible only to God. Patrick was later canonized by the Roman Church as a political move to control the Irish churches. He was thereafter known as "St. Patrick."

He has been known to have wrote the following inspiring statements:

"Christ beside me, Christ before me, Christ behind me, Christ within me, Christ beneath me, Christ above me"; and
*"If I be worthy, I live for my God to teach the heathen, even though they may despise me."*137

William Carey: (1761-1834)- Missionary to India.

Known as "The father of modern missions," William Carey was born at Northamptonshire, England, and became a cobbler at the age of 14. He studied privately on his own, and mastered Dutch, French, Greek and Hebrew before he was 20 years of age. Two years later, at the age of 22, he joined the Baptist church, and began preaching immediately, mostly on the theme of missions. He helped organize the English Baptist Missionary Society and was one of its first missionaries to India. His services there were remarkable for their range and depth.

In addition to soul-winning, Carey founded the Serampore College, and, with the aid of other linguists, he translated the Bible into 44 languages and dialects. Through his efforts, the Bible was made available to 300mill. people before the American Civil War.

He was also instrumental in developing grammars and dictionaries in Bengali, Sanskrit, and others.

David Livingstone: 1813-1873: Missionary to Africa

He was born near Glasgow, Scotland. He studied medicine and theology at the University of Glasgow. He tried to go to China as a missionary in 1838, but when the Opium War in China closed the doors, he went to Africa. He pushed 200 miles north of his assigned station and founded another mission station, Mebosta. Livingstone continued on the mission field and advanced 1400 miles into the interior in spite of the hardships he encountered. He was attacked and maimed by a lion; his home was destroyed during the Boer War; and his wife died on the field. Eleven years later, Livingstone was found by his bed, kneeling, and dead. Natives buried his heart in Africa, as he had requested, but his body was returned to Westminster Abbey in London.

George Lisle- (1750-1820)
Missionary to - Jamaica

Born in Virginia as the son of slaves Liele and Nancy, Lisle was boyhood friends with future Baptist minister David George. George Lisle was one of several thousand slaves who had to leave America with their masters, when their masters chose to emigrate as a result of the American War of Independence 1775-1783. George Lisle left with his wife, Hannah, and his four children. He became emancipated and preached on the racecourse at Kingston, Jamaica, where the novelty of a black itinerant ex-slave preacher attracted considerable attention. News of his itinerant-style preaching quickly spread. It was akin to the technique once used by Whitfield and equally successful. He was soon able to gather a congregation and purchase a piece of land about a mile from Kingston, where a chapel was gradually built.

To support his work, and expand it, George Lisle sought support from London. He was helped in this endeavor by Moses Baker, an Afro-European barber who arrived in Jamaica from America in 1783 and was baptized by Lisle on conversion to Christianity. A Quaker invited Baker to live on his estate and instruct the slaves in 'religious and moral principles'. To expand this educational work Moses Baker, like Lisle approached benefactors in Britain. He made contact with the Baptist, Rev. John Ryland, who became most interested in securing funds from British donors to meet such demand for missionary work, and was moved to helped instigate the non-denominational London Missionary Society to help provide for this.

Ryland's first missionary was funded by the Baptists rather than the LMS. Though sent to help, his missionary achievements were limited since he died early. Later, in the early 1800s, a trio of Baptist missionaries from Britain, Thomas Burchell, James Phillippo and William Knibb, and slightly later still others such as Samuel Oughton were more successful in supporting local African Baptist congregations and helping them develop their international links. However they met fierce resistance from the Planters who had great influence in the Jamaican House of Assembly, had provided adequately for their own spiritual needs with the Anglican authorities, and opposed both education and the congregational governance ideas of the Baptists, from being introduced amongst their slaves.

Adoniram Judson: (1788-1850) Missionary to BURMA:

Pioneer missionary to Burma. Adoniram Judson was the son of a Congregational minister. He taught himself to read at the age of three, and by his tenth year he knew Latin and Greek and was a serious student of theology. At the age of 16 he entered Brown University and was graduated three years later as the valedictorian of his class.

At Andover Theological Seminary he could not get away from the words of a missionary appeal, *"Go ye into all the world."* In 1810 he helped form the American Board of Commissioners for Foreign Missions; two years later, he and his new wife, Ann, sailed for India.

When the government refused to allow them to enter the country, they went to Burma, where they worked for six years before winning a convert. During those years they were plagued with ill health, loneliness, and the death of their baby son. Judson was imprisoned for nearly two years, during which time Ann faithfully visited him, smuggling to him his books, papers, and notes, which he used in translating the Bible into the Burmese language. Soon after his release from prison, Ann and their baby daughter, Maria, died of spotted fever.

Judson withdrew into seclusion into the interior, where he completed the translation of the whole Bible into Burmese.

In 1845 he returned for a visit to America, but the burning desire to win the Burmese people sent him back to the Orient, where he soon died.

As a young man, he had cried out, "I will not leave Burma, until the cross is planted here forever!" Thirty years after his death, Burma had 63 Christian churches, 163 missionaries, and over 7,000 baptized converts.

David Brainerd: (1718-1747)
Missionary to the American Indians.

David Brainerd was born April 20, 1718, at Hatham, Connecticut. His early years were spent in an atmosphere of piety though his father died when David was nine and his mother died five years later. As a young man he was inclined to be melancholy, with the welfare of his soul ever before him. His entire youth was divided between farming, reading the Bible, and praying
Early in life, he felt the call to the ministry and looked forward almost impatiently to the day when he could preach the Gospel. His formal education consisted of three years at Yale, where he was an excellent student until ill health forced him to return home. He completed his studies privately until he was fitted and licensed to preach by the Association of Ministers in Fairfield County, Connecticut. He turned down the offers of two pastorates in order to preach the Gospel to the American Indians. Jonathan Edwards wrote of him, "And, having put his hand to the plow, he looked not back, and gave himself, heart, soul, and mind, and strength, to his chosen mission with unfaltering purpose, with apostolic zeal, with a heroic faith that feared no danger and surmounted every obstacle, and with an earnestness of mind that wrought wonders on savage lives and whole communities."

Brainerd did his greatest work by prayer. He was in the depths of the forests alone, unable to speak the language of the Indians. But he spent whole days in prayer, praying simply that the power of the Holy Ghost might come upon him so greatly that the Indians would not be able to refuse the Gospel message. Once he preached through a drunken interpreter, a man so intoxicated that he could hardly stand up. Yet scores were converted through that sermon.

Plagued by ill health and the hardships of the primitive conditions, he died at the early age of 29, at the home of Jonathan Edwards, to whose daughter he was engaged. After his death, William Carey read his diary and went to India. Robert McCheyne read it and went to the Jews. Henry Martyn read it and went to India. Though it was not written for publication, his diary influenced hundreds to yearn for the deeper life of prayer and communion with God, and also moved scores of men to surrender for missionary work.

Count Nikolaus von Zinzendorf: (1700-1760) Moravian Founder and Missionary Leader-

The village of Herrnhut, means The Lord's Watch, (in present day Germany) came about because a little band of religious fugitives from Moravia (in the modern Czech Republic) asked Count Ludwig von Zinzendorf if they might settle on his land. The Count agreed. One Moravian leader was Christian David, a potter who burned with zeal for the Lord.

Zinzendorf, too, was a man of deep religious conviction and piety. At six he had written love letters to Christ. Deeply influenced by Francke and Spener's Pietism, the Count was only kept from becoming a minister by the raw exertion of family and state authority. Nonetheless, he and his wife had dedicated their lives completely to Christ. Eventually he would be chosen bishop of the Moravians. Zinzendorf was appalled at the divisions between churches and hungered to unite the different factions in a spiritual peace. At Herrnhut he learned what the Holy Spirit could accomplish in breaking down denominational walls.

Herrnhut had become a gathering place for many religious exiles. These spoke different languages and had differing customs. Creeds varied. Lutherans, Schwenkfelders, Separatists, Reformed and Brethren lived side by side. Squabbles developed. Zinzendorf found himself moving from home to home speaking with families of their spiritual need. The people began to study the Bible, hold all-night prayer vigils and confess their sins one to another. Zinzendorf established "bands," groups of two, three or more who would encourage each other spiritually. Plans were drawn up to reorganize and unify the community. A sense of expectancy grew.

On August 13, 1727, at a baptism and communion service, the Holy Spirit moved through the room. Differences dissolved. All embraced one another in forgiveness and a spirit of love. Christ became central to their thinking. They established a twenty-four hour around-the-clock prayer vigil which lasted one hundred years! The fervent prayers resulted in the sending out of missionaries to many lands--the first Protestant missions outside Europe and North America. Thus Herrnhut reached out and touched other lands. Moravians influenced John and Charles Wesley. Moravian missionary zeal prompted William Carey's efforts to reach India for Christ. "See what these Moravians have done," he said in his appeal to have missionaries commissioned.

Herrnhut was a busy and industrious place. Spinning, weaving, carpentry, pottery, farming and missionary training went on unceasingly. Each evening Zinzendorf selected a Scripture to be the watchword for the next day. Often he wrote a hymn to accompany the Word. Saturdays and Sundays were days of prayer and worship. Almost every day, each band met to exhort, reprove and pray for one another. Single women and single men lived in separate buildings. In a special home, the children of missionaries were cared for. Truly, Herrnhut became a remarkable experiment in Christian community as well as a major catalyst for Protestant missions.[138]

James Hudson Taylor: 1832-1905
(Missionary to CHINA:)

Pioneer missionary. James Hudson Taylor was born in Barnsley, England. He was the son of a Methodist minister. After studying medicine and theology, he went to China in 1854 as a missionary under the auspices of the China Evangelization Society. In 1858, after working in a hospital for four years, he married the daughter of another missionary. He returned to England in 1860 and spent five years translating the New Testament into the Ningpo dialect. He returned to China in 1866 with 16 other missionaries and founded the China Inland Mission. In 1870 his wife and two of their children died of cholera. He remained in China and before his death established 205 mission stations with 849 missionaries from England, and 125,000 witnessing Chinese Christians. He died in Changcha, China, in 1905.

C.T. Studd- 1860-1931
(English missionary to AFRICA:)

C.T. Studd was the son of a wealthy man, Edward Studd, who was converted to Christ under the ministry of Dwight L. Moody in 1877. Young C.T. Studd became an excellent cricket player, and at the age of 19 was captain of the team at Eton. He attended Cambridge University from 1880 to 1883, and, while he was there, he also heard Dwight L. Moody preach and was converted to Christ. Shortly afterwards, he and six other students dedicated their lives and their wealth to the Lord Jesus Christ and offered themselves to Hudson Taylor for work in China. They sailed to China in 1885.

In 1888 Studd married. He continued to work for several years before bad health forced him and his wife to return to England, where they turned over all their property to the China Inland Mission. Studd and his wife began to tour the world in order to raise funds for missions. While in southern India, on one of those tours, he found a suitable climate for him and his wife. He served there six years, after which time he returned to England to make plans to go to Africa.

In December of 1912 he left his family and was gone for two years in evangelistic work on the Dark Continent. He returned home for a short time, and then once again went back to Africa for five more years. Mrs. Studd did not join him until 1928, one year before she died. Studd died in Malaga, Africa, in 1931.

Alfred Buxton in the forward to the book entitled C.T. Studd: Cricketer & Pioneer by Norman Grubb states: "C.T.'s life stands as some rugged Gibraltar — a sign to all succeeding generations that it is worth while to lose all this world can offer and stake everything on the world to come. His life will be an eternal rebuke to easygoing Christianity. He has demonstrated what it means to follow Christ without counting the cost and without looking back."139

Perhaps one of C.T. Studd's greatest quotes which has been a challenge to many is:

"Some wish to live within the sound
of Church or Chapel bell;
I want to run a Rescue Shop
within a yard of hell."

John Hyde: (1865-1912) Missionary to India

John Hyde, better known as "The Praying Hyde," was born in Carrollton, Illinois. His father was a Presbyterian minister who faithfully proclaimed the Gospel message and called for the Lord to thrust out laborers into His harvest. He prayed this prayer not only in the pulpit but also in the home, around the family altar. This made an indelible impression on the life of young John, as he grew up in that atmosphere. John was graduated from Carthage College with such high honors that he was elected to a position on the faculty. However, he had heard the divine call to the regions beyond, and was not disobedient to the heavenly vision. He resigned his position and entered the Presbyterian seminary. In Chicago, he was graduated in the spring of 1892 and sailed for India the following October.

His ministry of prayer in India during the next 20 years was such that the natives referred to him as "the man who never sleeps." Some termed him "the apostle of prayer." But more familiarly he was known as "the praying Hyde." He was all these and more, for deep in India's Punjab, he envisioned his Master, and face to face with the eternal, he learned lessons of prayer which were amazing. Often he spent 30 days and nights in prayer, and many times was on his knees in deep intercession for 36 hours at a time.

His work among the villages was very successful, in that for many years he won four to ten people a day to the Lord Jesus Christ. Hyde was instrumental in establishing the annual Sialkote Conferences, from which thousands of missionaries and native workers returned, empowered anew and afresh for the work of reaching India with the Gospel.

Hyde's life of sacrifice, humility, love for souls and deep spirituality, as well as his example in the ministry of intercession, inspired many others to effect these graces in their own lives and ministries. He died February 17, 1912. His last words were, "Shout the victory of Jesus Christ!"

John Gibson Paton: (1824-1907) Missionary to New Hebrides, South Pacific.

John G. Paton was born in Dumfries, Scotland. His family later moved to Torthorwald, where, in a humble thatched cottage of three rooms, his parents reared five sons and six daughters. The middle room of the cottage was known as the "Sanctuary," for it was there that John's father went three times a day to pour out his heart in prayer to God for needs of his family.

At the age of 12, John was helping his father in the stocking business and also studying Latin and Greek. Later he left home to attend college in Glasgow, where he studied medicine and theology. Not long after, he became a missionary to the poor, degraded section of Glasgow. The work was discouraging, but during ten years of faithful labor, he won many to Christ, including eight boys, who later became ministers.

When John was about 30 years old, the Reformed Church of Scotland asked for a missionary to help with the work in the New Hebrides Islands. John answered the call, and soon he and his new bride were on their way to the South Pacific, in spite of the news that the previous missionaries had been murdered and eaten by the cannibals. The Patons settled on the island of Tanna, and began their ministry.

Since the natives had no written language, John talked to them in sign language. One day he learned a few native words, and after many months of labor, mastered their language and reduced it to writing. While there, his wife and infant son contracted tropical fever and died. The natives repeatedly stole his equipment, his life was in constant danger, but still he stayed and preached to them.

Moving to the island of Aniwa, Paton built a home, a mission house, two orphanages, a church, and a schoolhouse. And, after many years of patient ministry, he won the entire island to Christ! In 1899 he saw his Aniwa New Testament printed, and missionaries on 25 of the 30 islands of the New Hebrides. He went to heaven in 1907.

Jonathan Goforth: (1859-1936)
Missionary to China.

Jonathan Goforth was converted to Christ at the age of 18. While attending college, he did rescue mission work. He read Hudson Taylor's book about missionary work in China, and it so moved him that he dedicated his life to the Lord as a missionary. He and his wife labored in Honan, China; training hundreds of Chinese pastors and evangelists. During the Boxer Rebellion of 1900, the Goforths barely escaped with their lives, though suffering severe wounds. They returned to the Orient and helped start a revival in Korea in 1907. This revival seemed to follow them as they went back to China. In 1925 they went to Manchuria and served there for eight years before ill health forced them to return to Canada. Although Goforth was blind the last years of his life, he and his wife promoted missions until they went home to be with the Lord.

William Bramwell Booth:
(1829- 1912)
Founder of the Salvation Army.

William Booth was born in Nottingham, England. He was converted to Christ through the efforts of a Methodist minister, and soon became interested in working with the outcasts and the poor people of Nottingham. He preached on the streets and made hundreds of hospital calls before he was 20 years of age. From 1850 to 1861 he served as a pastor in the Methodist Church, after which time he and his wife left the church and stepped out by faith in evangelistic work in East London. It was there that he organized the East London Christian Revival Society. Out of this beginning came the Salvation Army, with its uniforms, organization, and discipline. By 1930 there were branches in 55 countries. Its main emphasis under General Booth was street preaching, personal evangelism, and practical philanthropy. More than 2,000,000 poor souls have professed faith in the Lord Jesus Christ through the work of the Salvation Army since its founding by the General.

Amy Carmichael: 1867- 1951
(Missionary to INDIA)

It was as if Jesus' words "Go ye" were spoken directly to her and the only option she had was to obey. Yet that obedience brought tremendous blessings to the hundreds of children and others to whom Amy Carmichael ministered in southern India. Prior to her life as a missionary, Carmichael had grown up in a prominent North Ireland family. Shortly after her father's death when she was 18, her family experienced financial pressures due to unpaid debts owed by her father's estate, and the family moved to Belfast. This was a providential move, for in Belfast Carmichael became involved in city mission work which awakened in her a desire for missionary service. Upon making her decision known to Mr. Wilson, the chairman of the Keswick Convention, he gave her his blessings, and Carmichael was on her way to the mission field.

Responding to God's call on her life, Carmichael headed for Japan at the age of 24. Working with the Keswick Convention, she took off running only to be halted by her health and the Japanese climate. It took her a little over a year to decide that God did not want her in Japan and she headed for Ceylon-without the prior approval of her board. She was not able to stay long though, since she was called back to Ireland to care for Mr. Wilson, her "second" father, who was seriously ill. Carmichael was a nonconformist from the start, yet a person of such fine character that it was hard to find a detractor among her fellow workers. Returning to the mission field after caring for Mr. Wilson, she arrived in Dohnavur, India, which would be her home for the next 55 years. It was there that she realized her life's work-rescuing children from the "secret" Hindu practice of temple prostitution.

Dohnavur Fellowship, the name of her organization, was soon actively involved in the rescue, care, feeding, and education of hundreds of children. She and her coworkers, primarily converted Indian women, adopted Indian dress and voluntarily forsook marriage for the sake of their work. This eventually became the Sisters of the Common Life-a Protestant religious order. The women were not bound by vows and could leave if they later decided to marry.

Though a serious fall left her an invalid, for the remaining 20 years of her life, Carmichael continued to appeal for her children and write books. She died in Dohnavur in 1951.

> *"I wish thy way. And when in me myself should rise, and long for something otherwise, then Lord, take sword and spear and slay."*
> - Amy Carmichael

George Leslie Mackay: 1844 – 1901 (pioneer Canadian Presbyterian missionary in northern Taiwan.)

Born near Zorra, Oxford County, Ontario, Canada, Mackay was christened by William Chalmers Burns, an English Presbyterian missionary to China, whose example inspired the younger man to become a missionary also.

A graduate of Princeton Theological Seminary, Mackay arrived in Taiwan in 1872 as the first foreign missionary of the western division of the Presbyterian Church in Canada. After consulting English Presbyterian missionaries already working in southern Taiwan, Mackay decided to establish his mission in the north with its headquarters at Tamsui (Danshui). He indefatigably conducted Christian work not only among the Chinese but also among the aboriginal populations.

In his evangelistic work, he was greatly assisted by his Chinese wife, Tui Chang Mia (Minnie Mackay), and by A. Hoa, his first convert and lifelong disciple. Mackay was a missionary entrepreneur skilled at raising funds to build churches and to found schools, the most important of which were Oxford College in Tamsui and a theological school that became Taiwan Theological College near Taipei. The Taiwanese referred to him as the Black-Bearded Barbarian of Formosa. He received an honorary D.D. from Queen's University in Kingston, Ontario, and his name is perpetuated by the Mackay Memorial hospital in Taipei.

The following books about his life and work are in my words, priceless! George Leslie Mackay, From Far Formosa: The Island, Its People, and Missions, J. A. Macdonald, ed. (1896). Marion Keith, The Black Bearded Barbarian (1912); R. P. MacKay, Life of George Leslie Mackay, D.D. 1844-1901 (1913); Duncan MacLeod, The Island Beautiful: The Story of Fifty Years in North Formosa (1923).

Victor Guy Plymire:
(Missionary to Tibet and China)

Victor Plymire was born January 10, 1881, to Amos and Laura Plymire in Loganville, Pennsylvania. He also had two brothers, Melvin (1872-1945) and Ralph (1892-1973) and a sister, Ethel, later Ethel Johnson (1889-1975). He committed his life to Christ at the age of fifteen at a street service. He went to school in Loganville and then worked for a time in electrical construction. But he felt a vocation for full-time Christian work. He became a minister of the Gospel Herald Society and pastored churches in Pennsylvania; in Philadelphia, Stroudsburg, Shamokin, and Scranton. He also attended the American Bible School of the Pentecostal Bands of the World and went to Christian and Missionary Alliance Institute at Nyack for a short time.

He felt a strong conviction that he was to be a missionary. He applied to the mission board of the Christian and Missionary Alliance and was accepted. He was sent to northwest China and left from Seattle, Washington, on February 4, 1908.

He had as a traveling companion Ivan Kaufmann, another missionary. He landed at Shanghai and then traveled on to Hankow (modern name Hankou, part of the triple city of Wuhan) and from there to Han Chung (modern spelling, Hanzhong) and from there to Tao Chow (modern spelling, Lintan) in the province of Kansu (modern spelling, Gansu). This town was to be his base.

Here, near the Tibetan border, he began to learn the language and to know the Tibetan people and customs. In October, 1912, he went to Sian (modern spelling, Xi'an) to meet and escort some missionaries to the Tibetan border. However, once he reached that city, fighting and turmoil that grew out of the proclamation of the Republic of China in 1911 made it unsafe to travel back to the border and the group went to Hankow. He was then asked to accompany another missionary who was ill back to the United States. Once there he stayed, reluctantly, for a furlough. Finally in

October, 1914, he left the United States and returned to Tao Chow. He became acquainted with Buddhist priests and visited several important monasteries, including Labrang in 1916 and Kum Bum. While there, as he did in other Tibetan communities and with merchant caravans, he preached and distributed tracts. On January 1, 1919, he married fellow missionary Grace Harkless in Min Chow (modern spelling, Min Xian) after an engagement of five years. They then returned to the United States for a furlough.

While on furlough, he and his wife began to go to Pentecostal services and received a baptism of the Spirit. He left the Christian and Missionary Alliance and was ordained into Assemblies of God in 1920. While on furlough he pastored the Assemblies of God church in Lancaster. During their time in Lancaster, the Plymire's son, John David, was born on July 13, 1921. The family sailed for Tibet in February of 1922.

Once in Tibet, Plymire established an Assemblies of God mission station at Tangar in the northeast part of the country. Tangar was also known as Donkyr or Hwangyuan. The modern name is Huangyuan. After all his years of ministry, Plymire first had the experience of a person converting to Christ under his ministry in 1924. After that the church in Tangar began to grow slowly. He was beginning to make plans for an expedition straight across Tibet to India, during which he would preach the Gospel in many remote locations. First, though, tragedy struck. First his son and then his wife died of smallpox in Jan., 1927.

Despite his grief, he continued to make plans for his expedition and set out on May 18, 1927. He went from Tangar to Lake Ko Ko (modern name, Qinghai), to Tsa Ka to across the Tsai Dam swamp (modern spelling, Qai Dam), through the Burhan Budhai Mountains to Danza Obo. Then he crossed the Dri River through the Tang La (modern spelling, Dang La) mountains to the Shiabden Gonpa monastery. For a time he preached near and possibly in the city of Lhasa and then went back to Shaibden Gonpa and westward through the mountains on to Cheri Ma Lung to Gartok (modern spelling, Garyarsa) to Ru Shuk (modern spelling, Rutog) near the Indian border on February 26,

1928. He had traveled 2,000 miles from northeastern through central to western Tibet. He then crossed into India and followed the Indus River into Leh, then on to Srinagar and eventually to Calcutta. On April 18, 1928, he sailed to Shanghai and then to Beijing. There he renewed his acquaintance with Ruth Weidman, a missionary who was doing language study. They were married on August 8, 1928, and a few weeks later, on September 3, they left for Tibet together with Ruth's sister, Elizabeth. They reached Tangar two months later. Victor had a heart attack in early 1930 that caused the Plymires to return to the United States on furlough early in that year. While in the United States, their son, David Victor, was born.

The Plymires returned to Tibet in October 1932, along with Elizabeth and her fiance, George Wood. In 1933 and 1934, Plymire visited the Kantsa tribe on evangelistic trips. In 1935 he again visited the monastery at Kum Bum. In 1936 he and his family were forced by fighting between the Kuo min tang and Communist forces to travel to Lanchow (modern spelling, Lanzhou) and were compelled to remain there until 1937, when they returned to Tangar. In 1937, also, their daughter Mary Ann (later Hawkes) was born. Victor's work consisted of assisting the growing church in Tangar and going on preaching expeditions, such as the one in 1941 to the monastery of Dulan in northern Tibet. In 1943, Ruth had a heart attack. She returned to the United States to recover and took the children with her. Victor left Tibet in September of 1945 to rejoin his family. He arrived home in Jan. of 1945.

After a two-year furlough, the Plymires left San Francisco for Tangar on February 14, 1947. Again they resumed their evangelistic work. In 1948, W. W. Simpson came to Tangar to hold evangelistic meetings. The next year, the war between the Kuo min tang and the Communists once again caused them to leave Tibet. They left Tangar to send their son and daughter to schools in the United States in June, 1949. While in Hong Kong, the news from the border made it clear that it would be unsafe to return for some time. The family returned to the United States and Victor eventually realized that because of the changed political situation, he would never be able to return to Tibet. The family settled in Springfield, Missouri, and he worked for the Assemblies of God missions board, preaching in various churches around the country and attending conferences, until his death on Dec. 8, 1956.

Charlotte "Lottie" Digges Moon
(1840 -1912) Missionary to China:

Lottie Moon—the namesake of the international missions offering—has become something of a legend. But in her time Lottie was anything but an untouchable hero. In fact, she was like today's missionaries. She was a hard-working, deep-loving Southern Baptist who labored tirelessly so her people group could know Jesus.

When she set sail for China, Lottie was 32 years old. She had turned down a marriage proposal and left her job, home and family to follow God's lead. Her path was not typical for an educated woman from a wealthy Southern family. But Lottie did not serve a typical God. He had gripped her with the Chinese peoples' need for a Savior.

For 39 years Lottie labored, chiefly in Tengchow and Pingtu. People feared and rejected her, but she refused to leave. The aroma of fresh-baked cookies drew people to her house. She adopted traditional Chinese dress, and she learned China's language and customs. Lottie did not just serve the people of China; she identified with them. Many eventually accepted her. And some accepted her Savior.

Lottie's vision was not just for the people of China. It reached to her fellow Southern Baptists in the United States. Like today's missionaries, she wrote letters home, detailing China's hunger for truth and the struggle of so few missionaries sharing the gospel with so many people—472 million Chinese in her day. She shared another timely message, too: the urgent need for more workers and for passionately supporting them through prayer and giving.

In 1912, during a time of war and famine, she buried herself in China's misfortunes, trying to help and no longer taking care of her needs. Her small cash reserves were gone. She gave and gave, not counting the cost to herself. She almost stopped eating. If others could not have food, neither would she. Her strength failed as Lottie silently starved, knowing that her beloved Chinese did not have enough food.

Her young colleagues, fearing for her life, sent for medical help, but the doctor's examination brought dire news. They felt her only hope for survival was to be returned to America. So, accompanied by a missionary nurse, Cynthia Miller, she embarked on the return voyage.

The ship docked in Kobe, Japan, one of Lottie's favorite places, to take on coal. On Christmas Eve 1912 she opened her eyes, smiled and looked around. With her last remaining strength, she raised her fists together—the fond Chinese greeting. She must have been greeting her Lord, for in that moment her spirit went out to meet Him.

John and Betty Stam: 1907-1934: (Missionaries to China)

Despite news of Chinese violence, both John and Betty responded to a request for workers from China Inland Mission. Betty met John at a CIM prayer meeting. They were attracted to each other, but they agreed that marriage might hinder their plans for service in China, so Betty left for China alone in 1931. John followed a year later. At his graduation from Moody Bible Institute, John urged his classmates to make sacrifices for God.

"The Great Commission was never qualified by clauses calling for advance only if funds were plentiful and no hardship or self-denial was involved," proclaimed John. "We are told to expect persecution, but with it victory in Christ. "When he arrived in Shanghai, John was delighted to see Betty, who had recently been forced to return for medical reasons. Their time together in Shanghai led to their engagement and marriage. The following year John and Betty served in Süancheng. Even though they didn't know the language very well, they always had a Chinese tract or Bible to hand out, and they gained many friends by their endearing and friendly manner. As their understanding of the language increased, John and Betty were able to spend more time proclaiming the Gospel. They were pleased to see the church in Süancheng grow as Chinese Christians began to take leadership roles.

In the fall of 1934, only weeks after the birth of their daughter, Helen Priscilla, John and Betty were assigned to the province of Anhwei. Missionaries had previously been evacuated from this station, but the Stams were assured that the area was reasonably safe from Communist threat.

But the situation had been misevaluated and within weeks of arriving, Communist soldiers were pounding at their gate. John, Betty and baby Helen were held captive, but John was permitted to send a letter to CIM. He must have known that they would likely be killed, but his letter shone with hope and contentment. He concluded with the words "may God be glorified whether by life or by death."

The next day the couple was forced to march to Tsingteh. Their captors paraded them before the townsfolk, who were amazed at John and Betty's calm expressions. One brave Chinese Christian dropped to his knees and begged for their release. John's last words were a plea for mercy for this brave man. Then with a swing of the sword, the Communists ended John and Betty's earthly lives, and placed them forever in the glorious presence of their Lord.

A Chinese pastor found little Helen thirty hours later, tucked in a sleeping bag. Ten precious dollars were hidden beside her-enough to get her to safety.

John and Betty spent but a few years in China before they were martyred, but their deaths stirred a revival for missions. Money poured in to mission agencies and a new generation of young people dedicated their lives to overseas service. Through their faith and dedication, John's last written wish was honored, and God was indeed glorified in life and in death.

> *"If the foreign field and the godless civilization about us call for the faithful planting of divine dynamite that will break stony hearts and save souls, the Church of Christ surely has a claim on our service."* - John Stam

HOWARD CARTER: (1891-1971)
(by Keith Malcomson)

Howard Carter was born in Birmingham, England into an unsaved but religious Anglican home. He had one younger brother called John. From an early stage he was marked by a speech impediment which brought ridicule at school. Their godly mother took them to church but it was not until he was nearly 20 years old that he began a real heart search for God and truth. He attended a service in a simple and humble Church of Christ building along with his brother. They were much touched by these people, soon they both received Christ as Savior and were baptized in water. A member of this congregation soon had these two brothers helping with the YMCA who went out preaching to the poor, reading the Scriptures, singing, and witnessing. This was their training ground.

This same man took them to Friday night meetings where they were taught about being filled with the Spirit and of God's power to heal. Soon they saw their mother healed from kidney trouble and crippling arthritis. One man from this fellowship was the first Pentecostal they had met. He deeply affected them with his fervent spirit, his inspirational preaching and his continual praising of Christ. Soon they attended their first Pentecostal meeting where believers spoke in (other) tongues; all this they readily received as in accordance with the New Testament.

They accompanied these new friends in 1912 to the Sunderland Whitsuntide Convention where (preachers), Boddy, Wigglesworth, Barratt and others ministered. They were in awe of the clear powerful preaching and the beautiful singing in (other) tongues. After trying to bring this great blessing back to the Church of Christ they were quickly dismissed of their membership.

The next two years they attended this conference hearing speakers from Germany, Holland, Norway, Switzerland, America and Britain. Many laid hands upon them to receive the Baptism but still they did not receive, Howard was holding unto strong views that you did not need to speak in tongues to be baptized in the Spirit. In 1915 they attended a convention in Bedford, while kneeling to pray he was mightily caught up in the Lord and without realizing, was making a great noise and disturbing the meeting. The Pastor asked an elder to take this noisy brother to the vestry. As he crossed the threshold he broke forth in tongues for the first time. The cross and the atonement seemed so much more wonderful and a deep consciousness of the Lord's presence was his from then on. It was not long before he was left with responsibility of pastoring this small flock in Birmingham which soon started to grow.

Feeling the call of God he moved to part time work and gave himself to the study of God's Word. When approached by a brother who would pay his way at a Bible college he turned down this offer feeling he must trust the Lord totally. He then resigned work altogether just leaving a box at the back of the church for offerings. When war came in 1916 he was imprisoned as a conscientious objector in Wormwood Scrubs, London and later at Dartmoor. He was fed on bread and water, his hair cropped off, was made to wear prison clothes and locked in a cell by himself. It was at this time that he became absorbed in studying the nine gifts of the Holy Ghost. It was during secluded times of prayer and study that God opened to him a beautiful revelation of these nine distinct gifts which he would later teach across the world. In 1918 at the end of the war he returned to Pastor the Church in Birmingham. From this time forward he was greatly used in the gifts of interpretation of tongues, prophecy and the word of wisdom.

Reluctantly after much (spiritual) wrestling, he answered a call to London and stepped out with a word from the Lord which said: "Gather my people together and build for me. A great company shall come and ye shall build for me. And there shall be heaps of money..." He started by purchasing a building in London and held an opening campaign with George Jeffreys as the speaker. Out of this a strong work was established. He was then approached by a

Mr.Mundell who believed he was to be the new principal of the PMU Bible School now in Hampstead. Howard felt he was mistaken, but after an hour of persuasion he finally consented to fill the gap for a couple of months until a suitable man was found. In February 1921 at the age of thirty he took this responsibility.

Just 18 months later the PMU informed him that due to lack of funds they were going to close this school. Howard and the students prayed fervently, then he offered to take on the full responsibility of the work and finances. Progressively, other gifted teachers were added such as C.L. Parker and Harold Horton.

By 1925 there were 40 staff and students and those students had come from England, Scotland, Ireland, Wales, Norway, Sweden, Holland and Switzerland. In 1924 Harold was one of the 13 founding members of Assemblies of God and soon one of seven elected members. The School, although remaining independent, did become a recognized part of the AG. In 1925, he was invited on the missionary council and also took over the running of the Friday night rallies at Sion College from Polhil. During this time, he exercised great faith to see the financial needs met. In 1926, he started the School Evangelistic society, pushing the students out to start new works. He purchased buildings around the country where these laborers could minister. Next came a women's Bible School, then a Bible Correspondence Course. From this Bible School, missionaries went forth to China, Japan, Korea, Ceylon, Africa, Egypt, Palistine, Russia and many other nations. In Great Britain over 140 evangelists and pastors were now laboring and the correspondence course had students in five continents.

In 1934, the call came to go minister in America, which led into his first world tour starting with just 5 pounds in his pocket... Over the next two years he traveled 150,000 miles through about 30 different countries, visiting every British AoG missionary and many others. He faced death, danger and hardship in every manner, but saw multitudes saved, healed and baptized in the Holy Ghost, including 19 missionaries. This was the first of 3 such trips which came to an end at the beginning of the war in 1939.

William F.P. Burton (1886-1971):
Missionary to The Congo
(by Keith Malcomson)

Born in Liverpool in 1886 he came from a strong Christian background. His parents had dedicated him to God's work in Africa even before he was born and as he grew servants of the Lord had laid hands on him with a prayer that God would send him to preach the Gospel in Africa. It was under the preaching of R.A.Torrey at Evangelistic services in London that he first come under deep conviction of sin and came to the Lord in 1905.

From the very beginning he was sold out (committed). His new life started with regular Bible study and the winning of souls to Christ. He was one of Myerscough's young men who was blessed to be taught by him the Word of God for some five years continuously. It was in 1909 that they first heard of the outpouring at Azuza St. in Los Angeles. Until then he had not understood the meaning of the (unknown) tongues he had heard of back in 1906 in Welsh revival meetings. At the convention in 1911 at Preston, he received his much sought for Baptism of fire. After this, when the PMU Bible school opened he eagerly joined himself to it. This led to a life of living by faith. He spent the next three years traveling the countryside preaching in homes and the open-air as well as pastoring a little assembly at Lytham and helping Myerscough at the Preston Bible School.

While standing in a butcher shop in a small English village, he was prompted of God to lay hands on a deaf lady in Jesus name and she was instantly healed. All of the village quickly heard and this led to a revival in two quarrelling Methodist Churches, which had not seen one soul saved in 11 years between them. In confirming his missionary call, God answered prayer by miraculously giving him a third set of teeth. All this was great preparation for the mission field.

During this time, C.T. Studd was planning to go to the Congo (Africa) and suggested Willie go with him, but he had no witness that this was the Lord. He set sail for Africa in 1914, the following year he was joined by Jimmy Salter (who later married Smith Wigglesworth's daughter). This work would eventually be called the Congo Evangelistic Mission. These were early days of fighting sickness, encountering cannibal tribesmen, learning the language and making the first maps of the country. As they went forth preaching, God confirmed His Word with signs following and souls saved. Just after their initial arrival in 1915, the work commenced in the healing of a local native who was badly bent over and walking with sticks. Instantly he was healed and continued with a straight back for the next 33 years.

In 1918, Burton traveled to South Africa in order to recruit more missionaries; the first and most willing was Hettie, who became his wife. A special week of meetings were called in 1920, 160 of the converts gathered. Divisions and disputes were coming in amongst the converts and as yet none had received the Holy Ghost. But at these meetings under strong preaching, great conviction of sin came amongst them and amidst brokenness and repentance the Spirit of God was outpoured, all were filled and empowered for service. The work grew quickly during the 1920's and more missionaries came to help.

He was on the field until 1960 when independence for Congo meant him leaving. In some notes from the year 1962 he writes, "For 57 years I have been preaching and giving Bible talks. Since escaping from the Congo, 2 years ago, I have given Bible-talks almost every night. I love feeding Gods flock, because I love Him. It is a passion with me to give out the blessed truths that I glean from His Word." By the time of his death in 1971 there had been about 2000 native churches raised up and he could have well said, "Truly the signs of an apostle were wrought among you in all patience, in signs, and wonders, and mighty deeds." (Interestingly), it was on the very same day that both Burton and Howard Carter (another great Pentecostal pioneer) went to be with the Lord.

Philip James Elliot:
Missionary to Ecuador (1927-1958)

Jim Elliot, a modern martyr, gained international recognition when he died with four others at the hands of Auca Indians. His story and memoirs have become a source of missionary inspiration through the writing and speaking of his wife, Elisabeth. Born of Scottish ancestry in Portland, Oregon to a farmer-evangelist family, Jim became a Christian at the tender age of six after a church meeting one night. Faith afterwards became an integral part of his everyday life.

After high school he enrolled in Wheaton College in 1945, five years junior to Billy Graham. He first met his future wife there, much like Mr. Graham did Ruth Bell. Those were formative years for Jim, not just academically but also spiritually. He was most inspired by the writings and life story of Amy Carmichael, with whom he felt a kindred spirit.

Graduating from Wheaton, he quickly discovered a vocation in the missionary life. The field he chose was the unexplored frontiers of Ecuador in Latin America. Not content with bringing the Gospel to the civilized people of the country, he and his four companions flew their MAF Piper plane over the lands of the savage Auca tribe. Their first landing meant a tragic massacre, but out of that seemingly senseless tragedy comes a great testimony of the call of God on one man's life.

He was survived by his wife and his daughter Valerie who was only a baby at the time. Elisabeth Elliot went on to write such moving chronicles of her husband's life as "Shadow of the Almighty" and "Strange Ashes." These have inspired and challenged numerous people along the years for a closer walk in service to the LORD.

Scott Wesley Brown, a musicianary (musician missionary) wrote the following song after reading "Shadow of the Almighty" (Elisabeth Elliot) and "Lords of the Earth" (Don Richardson). May we be challenged by it to higher levels of devotion to our God.

HE IS NO FOOL

I have lost track of all the Sundays
The offering plates gone by
And as I gave my hard earned dollars
I felt free to keep my life
I talk about commitment
And the need to count the cost
But the words of a martyr show me
I do not really know His cross

Chorus:
For he is no fool
Who gives what he cannot keep
To gain what he cannot lose
Yes, he is no fool
Who lays his own life down
I must make this the path I choose

Obedience and servanthood
Are traits I have rarely shown
And the fellowship of His sufferings
Is a joy I have barely known
There are riches in surrendering
That can't be gained for free
God will share all heaven's wonders
But the price He asks is me.

137 www.quotes-museum.com
138 Christian History Institute
139 C.T. Studd: Cricketer & Pioneer by Norman Grubb

Chapter Eleven

~

In the Present-
"Making History"

In addition to the biographies of great missionaries of old, I now wish to highlight the lives and work of individuals who are continuing to labor in the mission field at the present time.

The following ministers are by no means the only ones working in foreign missions today. These, however, are personal acquaintances of mine who have initiated a mission work and have agreed to write a brief biography of themselves and their work in missions. These, and all others who have given their lives to the spreading of the gospel to the heathen of this world, are the bona fide heroes of our day! Success is not determined by the amount in ones bank account, the size of ones property, or how many cars they own, but by whether a person has obeyed the Lord or not. God help the church to keep a right perspective on life!

Nate Saint, fellow missionary who died with Jim Elliot at the hands of the feared Auca Indians, once wrote: "And people who do not know the Lord ask why in the world we waste our lives as missionaries. They forget that they too are expending their lives...and when the bubble has burst they will have nothing of eternal significance to show for the years they have wasted."140 Dear reader, please peruse carefully the following pages, and as you do, "whisper" a prayer for these missionaries lives, families, and work for Christ, realizing that you are praying for a most worthy cause.

> "We who have Christ's eternal life need to throw away our own lives." - George Verwer

AMOS CHIN: Burma
(Myanmar)

Amos Chin is a Holiness Preacher from the country of Burma (Myanmar). This Asian nation has roughly 52 Million people, the majority of which are Buddhist. Although things have improved slightly over the past years, Myanmar remains a nation in deep crisis. The harsh military regime refuses to relinquish governmental control to the rightfully elected leader, and a bloody civil war continues to devastate the nation.

Rev. Chin received a vision from the Lord to start a holiness Pentecostal church movement while training for the ministry in a Bible College in India. Soon after he had completed his studies, he spent most of his time traveling and conducting revival and evangelistic meetings. He encountered much hardship as an itinerant preacher. On one occasion he was imprisoned for nearly a year for his faith and for witnessing to a Buddhist Monk. In spite of the poverty, oppression from the government, imprisonment and hunger, he was not deterred in the least bit! Instead, he continued to pursue the vision God had given to him.

For four consecutive years, Amos Chin attempted to start a church in Burma, but without success. Again, however, he did not allow circumstances to cause him to quit. He truly believed that God would open the door and allow him to plant many churches in his homeland. After spending much time in prayer and fasting, he began to see a breakthrough. Souls began to receive his message and he was now able to organize a small home cell group.

The Bible Missionary Church, as his group is known, came into existence from this small group of new believers in 1997. By 2006, and by the grace and the providence of God, there were 35 established churches and 10 mission outreach centers, which will eventually be established congregations with their own building. The Bible Missionary Church also operates 35 orphanages. Many children are

THE SPRINKLE OF NATIONS

abandoned in Myanmar due to severe poverty and the parent's inability to financially take care of their children.

*Amos Chin
interpreting for
Dr. C.S. Pahlman*

Dr. William Hill and I have ministered in Myanmar several times, working under the leadership of Rev. Chin. Dr. Hill and I will both attest to the fact that Amos Chin is a godly man, full of compassion and conviction.

Holiness Convention in Kale; Myanmar-2004

Rev. Chin gained a greater appreciation for Biblical holiness standards after reading a copy of Dr. Hill's book entitled *What is Holiness?* while in India. I am not certain how he obtained Dr. Hill's book while visiting India. God's plans and purposes are amazing! One thing is certain; the Lord made it possible for Amos Chin to read the book and make contact with Dr. Hill and invite him to conduct crusades and conventions in Myanmar, which have proven to be a great blessing to the saints there.

Most recently (May 2008), Myanmar has experienced one of the strongest Cyclones to ever hit that region. Cyclone Nargis was the deadliest named cyclone in the North Indian Ocean Basin, as well as the second deadliest named cyclone of all time, behind Typhoon Nina of 1975. One aid worker has claimed that the death toll from the cyclone and its aftermath may reach 300,000; if this is correct, Nargis would be the 2nd deadliest cyclone ever. The Bible Missionary Church has used this tragedy as a means to reach the Burmese with the gospel message. They have taken several teams of gospel workers into the Irrawaddy Delta to feed and cloth the poor as well as to preach salvation to the lost and hurting. Many positive stories to being reported of many coming to saving faith in Christ by these humble efforts.

Cyclone Nargis relief by Bible Missionary Church (2008)

JOSHUA A. AJEIGBE:
Ilesa, Nigeria
(Written by: J. B. Ayodeji and edited by C.S. Pahlman)

Evangelist J.A. Ajeigbe was born in the 1950's to the family of Pastor Daniel Ajeigbe and his wife Beatrice. Pastor Ajeigbe was one of the pioneers of the great awakening of the 1930 that saw revival spread across the West African region with an "epicenter" at Ilesa, Osun State, Nigeria.

HIS CONVERSION EXPERIENCE:

While still a youth, Joshua was fasting and praying, seeking for an experience with God. Through the reading of Scriptures such as Psalm 51 and James 5:16, the Holy Spirit brought a wave of conviction of sin upon him that resulted in sound salvation that pitched him against sin with a perfect hatred and allied him with true righteousness and perfect love. Subsequent to this salvation were the experiences of sanctification and a Holy Ghost baptism.

HIS MARRIAGE AND FAMILY:

He is married to his darling wife Mary, who he fondly calls Mrs. FAR (Far Above Rubies: Proverbs. 31:10). They are blessed with several beautiful and godly children.

His ministerial life:

Gripped with a heart burden for the revival of the Church and bringing back the day of heroic Christianity in Nigeria and beyond, he feels as if he was called into the ministry to pursue this mission of the Church's revival and the evangelization of the world in the end-time.

He certainly thanks God for how He has helped him to see this vision realized with the birth of his ministry he named the Holy Ghost Revival Mission. It started in 1987. The Holy Spirit School of Evangelism was then begun in 1989; after that the Mission Nigeria in 1992, which inaugurated for the purpose of rallying God's people around God's plan for this generation.

Rev. Ajeigbe then had a passion to launch a ministry called Youth With A Vision in the year 1999. This movement is for the purpose of raising Christian youths to reach the world of other young people. Then came the birth of what is named The Teachers Special in 2002. This was meant to renew the vision of child training and to facilitate the moral transformation of our decadent youth and children in this age. In 2005, Rev. Ajeigbe began a marriage ministry simply called Husband & Wife Program; this he says has the purpose of restoring the family and home.

After this, the emergence of Obadiah Outreach came into existence with the sole purpose to reach and inspire the true Christians in Government establishments to reach their colleagues for Jesus Christ.

Finally, the vision God gave him for the Theophilus Project became a reality recently. This ministry is meant to reach the high ranking government officers in his homeland of Nigeria

HIS INVOLVEMENT IN MISSION WORKS:

Because of the ministries that God has enabled him to establish, Joshua Ajeigbe has developed a greater desire for Christian missions. From year 1987 he began to organize conferences for ministers in which he called The Fire Conference. These have been occasions to share the burden of revival and the need for spiritual fire among Christians and their ministers, as well as a heavy emphasis on the evangelization of the lost souls of the world.

In the year 1993, Rev. Ajeigbe began to explore the genuine spiritual needs of the entire country of Nigeria. He had the vision of evangelizing the whole nation with the gospel of Christ. With much passion, he made a successful effort to mobilize home missionaries to visit all of the local government areas in the thirty-six states that make up Nigeria. This was a mission to ascertain the spiritual situation of the people of the whole land. It was discovered that there were local governments (towns and cities) that were entirely without any Christian church.

OSUN LANDMARK CONFERENCE 2004:

This was a gathering of Revivalist ministers in Osun State towards a "rebirth" of Evangelism in Osun State. Dr. Rev. Hill and Mrs. Hill remained in Nigeria during this week to address the audience. The conference came up the week after Nigeria 2004. Some ministers who missed Nigeria 2004, seized the opportunity of the landmark conference. Most of the LGA's in Osun State participated in this Conference.

MILESTONE 2006 FEB. 16 – 25, 2006:

In the steady effort to mobilize the Nigeria Church to evangelize the northern part of the nation of Nigeria, another great conference tagged Milestone 2006 was held in February 2006. The aim of Milestone 2006 was to bring the days of heroic Christianity back to Nigeria and regain Pentecost. Participants were drawn from more than half of the local government areas in the nation with many of them sponsored. Apart from several ministers of God who labored with Evangelist Ajeigbe to see the program succeed, four powerful holy men of God came from USA to minister in the ten day Christian Congress. They are Dr. W. F. Hill, Rev. Rev. James V. Collins, Dr. Charles Pahlman, and Rev. Gary Hampton.

Nigeria 2004 Minister's Conference

CONCLUSION:

Evangelist Joshua A. Ajeigbe is a man of vision, a vision to see the true Church revived so as to be engaged in fruitful soul-winning efforts and missions that shall see the world evangelized. The vision is for a worldwide revival and the winning of souls with Nigeria as the launching pad. The undeviating theme is reviving the church towards reaching the lost. Joshua Ajeigbe has authored numerous books that have been a great blessing to many in Africa and beyond.

REV.E.ADE.SHOBANKE

(Abeokuta, Nigeria:)
written   by   his   son
Emmanuel Shobanke)

Rev.E.Ade.Shobanke is a Nigerian evangelist and pastor. The Lord saved him as a young man and soon called him into the ministry. Ade Shobanke is a man with a great vision for God's work, and has stood by his calling through many tests and trials.

During his calling to the pastorate, he had a prophetic dream in which he was distributing water to a large number of people at an extreme end of the city of Abeokuta in Southern Nigeria. It should be stated that in many of these communities, it is difficult to find clean drinking water. Many people are sickly and some die due to the lack of good water. In the dream, as he was sharing the water to the people he was asking God the reason why so many people were there, and God told him that the reason is that the water that they had was polluted. The Lord then said that the water that he was giving them was living water! The dream had a spiritual application. The people did not only need clean drinking water because they only had polluted water; but that they also needed the clean and wholesome Word of God, which the Bible calls Living Water! The people needed the gospel of Jesus Christ. Even the churches that profess Christ had become polluted with liberalism and apostasy! They needed a preacher of righteousness to visit them and provide them with truth and genuine power. This they found in the man Ade Shobanke.

The vision that God gave to him was expanded to the training of young men and women to be a preachers and teachers of the true Word of God. After establishing a church in Abeokuta, the Lord led Rev. Shobanke to launch a holiness Bible school here as well. Over the years, many have been trained and equipped to minister the gospel, by God's grace numerous ones have graduated and have gone on to preach all over the this large African nation.

In front of Rev. Shobanke's church sign

HISTORY OF CHRIST AMBASSADORS HOLINESS CHURCH:

Rev. E. Ade Shobanke is a native of Lagos State, Nigeria. After his conversion to Christ, he left his well paying government job and decided to attend a conservative Bible College in Nigeria. From the Bible school he became an evangelist ministering the good news all around the large city of Lagos, as well as preaching a few times in other countries of the world. The time came when the Lord revealed to him the vision mentioned above. Abeokuta was a smaller city compared to Lagos, but the sin and evil was great. The worship of idols is common to these pagan people. Rev. Shobanke was one of the first Bible Evangelists to bring the full Gospel of Jesus Christ to this territory.

The church began as a house fellowship in his small living room. After several years, it grew to about ten members. Some of these attendees had come with him from Lagos and joined him in a soul winning effort. The problem that arose was that a building was needed if they were to continue to grow. Finances, however, were a real obstacle due to the declining Nigerian economy. It was during this time that he met his wife to be. God blessed their marriage and gave them four beautiful and godly children, two boys and two girls.

Minister's Conference Feb. -2008

After their marriage, God began to greatly bless his ministry. The Lord provided a small church building that held nearly 100 members. Several years later, God gave them two plots of land elsewhere in Abeokuta where they built the Bible school: CHRIST AMBASSADORS HOLINESS BIBLE COLLEGE. Soon after, the Lord promised Rev. Shobanke a bigger church. In 1995, God gave them ten plots of land on which they built a church sanctuary, a prayer tower, two dormitories, and a children's fellowship hall; all of this capable of holding over 1500 people! Included on this land is a field that is used for outdoor crusades. God has gloriously provided for this thriving ministry of E. Ade Shobanke.

The Lord has been likewise blessing this work with miraculous signs and wonders; many people have received physical healing, as was promised by Christ in His Great Commission to the church. Every first Friday night of each month, the church conducts a Healing Night; it is here that they have witnessed many miracles to the glory of God.

E. Ade Shobanke has a heart for Bible Holiness and promotes and defends such standards in his church. In the Abeokuta church an Annual Holiness Camp meeting is held. Numerous Holiness ministers from the United States have been invited to preach these camp meetings as well as other revivals; among them are Dr. Bill Burkett, Dr. William Hill, Lloyd Shuecraft, Darryl Meadow, Davy Boggs, and Dr. Charles Pahlman.

In 1977 God performed a wonderful miracle through Pastor Shobanke for the Nigerian Conservative Christians. At this time, there was no one willing to print Bibles based on the King James Version text in Yoruba, the main Nigerian language. The only one available at this time was a Yoruba Bible based on the Good News Bible, a very poor translation of the original text of Scripture. It was while reading a magazine from Rev. M.A. Dauod's ministry (International Bible Association, Dallas Texas) that Rev. Shobanke was impressed by the Lord to write M.A. Daoud about the possibility of printing them King James Version Bibles in their language.

Rev. Daoud wrote back but the answer was not what Rev. Shobanke wished to hear. He would have to come up with half of the money before the printing of the Bibles would begin. The rest of the money would be due before they would ship them to Nigeria.

Rev. Shobanke did not have the finances needed to print the 25,000 Bibles that they were desiring. He immediately replied to MA Daoud that "...money was not the problem, but needing the right version of the Bible in Yoruba is their chief problem". What he meant by this was that they did not have the money to print and ship the Bibles, but that God knew the need and that He would some how miraculously provide. Rev. Shobanke felt like he was stepping out in faith when he wrote Rev. Dauod this second time.

This second letter so inspired Rev. Daoud that after he read it he began the printing of the Bible without receiving one dollar or naira. Evidently, God moved upon MA Daoud to print the Bibles by faith, trusting that the money would be provided by another source. To God be the glory!

When the printing of these thousands of Yoruba Bibles was complete, God raised up a Christian businessman in Nigeria who had heard about the need who then helped to pay for them. These Bibles have been distributed throughout this vast country and only eternity will reveal how many were saved and discipled by them. Hudson Taylor, the missionary to China said it best: ""When God's work is done in God's way for God's glory, it will not lack for God's supply."

Rev. E. Ade Shobanke's future ministry work is dedicated to evangelizing every part of Abeokuta. It is the desire of his heart to see a revival break out all over his home town and then to flow out to other cities and countries in Africa and ultimately around the world.

Rev. Bockarie & Clarissa Mansaray: (Freetown, Sierra Leone West Africa)- written by Rev. Mike Johnson

Sierra Leone has been given the lowest rank of all the countries of the world according to the normalized measure of life expectancy, literacy, education and standard of living. It has also been considered the seventh lowest on the Human Poverty Index, according to studies developed and released by the United Nations.

During the time of John Newton, author of that great hymn Amazing Grace, Sierra Leone was an important center of the transatlantic slave trade. Many more years would pass before formerly enslaved African Americans and West Indians would be received into Freetown, the nation's capital and largest city. It is here at the foot of the ancient and famed cotton tree many fortunate souls would officially be set free.

It was in this very city God determined to set a young man free from sin just five years before their dreadful civil war. Bockarie Immanuel Mansaray came to know the Lord in September of 1986 at a Bible School under the late missionary, George Cover. In that same week he responded to the call of God to preach and started a church in his own house. After only a few months, Rev. Cover, recognizing him to be a promising young man, began to involve Bockarie in the ministry.

While attending the Pentecostal Bible College, Bockarie met and later married his wife Clarissa. It was soon clear that God had greater things in store for the furtherance of His kingdom through this union. Feeling it was the Lord's will for them to branch off into full time pastoral work, the Mansarays took the step of faith in obedience to God, and He led them into bigger and better things. It would not happen overnight however.

The early years of their marriage were faced head on with extreme poverty just like those around them to whom they were called. With no support from the outside, they pressed on with prayer and fasting. They visited and prayed with people and continued to preach the Word of God faithfully, and the Lord began to give them a wonderful harvest. God blessed Elim International Worship Center even in the midst of a great civil war which forced missionaries to flee the country for their own safety. Five years after the start of their civil war Elim International Christian Academy opened its doors; ten years after the church began the week of his conversion. The final battle would find them positioned right in the midst of a most frightful conflict in Freetown. With rebels on the one side, allied forces on the other, and bombs passing overhead from both directions, the Lord sheltered them from any harm. To God be the glory!

Pastor Mike Johnson addressing Christian School students in Freetown.

It has not been an easy journey, but the hand of the Lord moves with faithful labor. The need for space continues to be an obstacle as enrollment in the school continues to increase. With partnership from saints in the United States a much needed building was erected to meet the need. The initial enrollment of eighteen children in the first year has grown to over three hundred in the 2007-08 school terms. The school will expand another grade level each year until it is complete from Kindergarten through grade twelve with a projected enrollment of over four hundred young people for the 2008-09 school terms. This is a tremendous evangelistic outreach as even Muslim parents are among those enrolling their children so as to keep their young ones from having to attend the public school system... and these children are required to attend church at Elim International Worship Center!

My first meeting with Rev. Bockarie was at the bus station when, at the request of Pastor William Hill, he came to minister in my church in the spring of 2005. I caught the vision, and that December had the privilege of traveling to Freetown for the first time to participate in the Great Leadership Conference and Revival. Our team taught pastors and church leaders during the morning into the afternoon and preached evangelistic services in the evenings. In February of 2008 I returned alone to teach and preach the same meeting. What a joy to see the number of pastors and leaders coming daily for a full week of teaching, and to see the church packed each night of the revival with benches even set in the courtyard for lack of space inside.

While we are grateful for what God has done, we eagerly anticipate what He is yet to do. Fourteen home cell groups have effectively expanded the influence of Elim International Worship Center. These smaller groups come together for a much larger combined rally the first Sunday of each month. There are two group leaders per home cell group, and each one is personally trained and equipped by Pastor Bockarie before being assigned their area of ministry. This effective means of outreach currently touches between 400-500 souls weekly. Rev. Mansaray's vision is to increase the number of home cells to at least twenty for the purpose of planting churches throughout the city. Through the means of the annual Great Leadership Conference he seeks to train ministers to go into the twelve provinces of

Sierra Leone in an effort to fulfill Christ's great commission to the Church in their Jerusalem as well as their Judea and Samaria. I am delighted to take part in such a work!

-- *Bro. Bockarie's ministry building in Freetown*

Linda Tobman: (Taiwan)

Linda Tobman, who was already a grandmother and widow, graduated from Free Gospel Bible Institute in 1993. She left for Taiwan that same summer arriving with only $475 US in her pocket. At this point, she did not know where she was going to live, did not know how to change or spend the money or even to buy food to eat. She had gained a burden for this predominately Buddhist country while yet in Bible School. God providentially sent a young married couple from this small island nation of Taiwan to Free Gospel Bible Institute the same year Linda Tobman was there. Joe and Lana (as they were known in the U.S.) shared their burden and the need for Christian workers in their homeland. It is estimated that the country is 96% Buddhist. Linda Tobman began to pray for the needs of Taiwan, and to her amazement, God ended up calling her to go there as a missionary!

Trusting only in the Lord that He would provide her every need, she launched out into the work God had called her to. Soon after arriving, she realized that she was in a world totally different than what she was accustomed to in the USA. She was alarmed and deeply sorrowed to see the way people lived and the devotion they gave to their idols and false gods. Through many prayers and tears she asked God how she could reach so many people for Him being only one person. She came to realize that God's arms were reaching out even farther than she was and that He would show her the way. Linda Tobman began her work in central Taiwan at the Four Square Gospel Church of Taichung, Taiwan, where Pastor Tong was the pastor. She worked teaching Sunday School, adult Bible classes, and became a leader of the youth fellowship. After four years, a burden was put in her heart to begin an outreach ministry to the many people who gathered at the city park. One Sunday in the springtime, she took her Sunday School class to the Taichung public park and observed many people watching and listening to the Easter lesson she was teaching there. The park was filled with many kinds of people: prostitutes, homeless people, young and elderly people, run-a-ways from the Philippines, Buddhist monks, Moonies, Mormons, Jehovah Witnesses, and others. She ministered to them as the Lord brought them her way, primarily through songs and preaching.

Due to her growing awareness of the spiritual need, she began a Bible study in her home in 1997. This small gathering of hungry Christians eventually grew into a church congregation that met regularly on Sunday nights. She named the place of worship Holiness Pentecostal Church. The congregation was made up of both Chinese and Filipino worshipers. Linda Tobman preached there for several years, during which time she witnessed numerous people saved and filled with the Holy Ghost according to Acts 2:4.

After being in Taiwan about five years, Taiwan Ministries became a legal organization and a board was formed with herself as president, Charles Pahlman as vice president, and Scott Johnson as secretary and treasurer. By this time, her ministry consisted of city park ministry, Bible studies, summer camps for children and youth, teaching English (using the Bible), tract distribution, and speaking engagements in many different churches.

At the present time, her work in Taiwan has been on going for over fifteen years. Through Taiwan Ministries, several graduates of Free Gospel Bible Institute have come to work on the Island of Taiwan. These individuals are involved in pastoring and various ministry tasks in different areas across the Island.

Linda Tobman, at the age of sixty- two, is now ministering and living in the central mountain town of Chung-Liao. It is a busy life for her as she reaches out to the Buddhist and Taoist children and adults with the Word of God. She teaches Bible and English, charging nothing for her services. She has three children's classes going at the same time, with the help of her coworker, among them being a national worker named Grace Chiu.

Linda Tobman preaches every other Sunday morning and participates in the Thursday prayer meeting in her mountain church under the leadership of Pastor Peter Hsu. She works together with other Christians in her church going to the homes of her students and friends on Tuesday nights for a home worship. During this time the Spirit of the Lord has reached out to those that will not attend church regularly, it is in services like this that many in the villages can hear and see the joy that true Christians have as they worship Jesus.

Since coming to Taiwan, Linda Tobman has witnessed numerous miracles. She claims that one man who had never been in a church before accepted the Lord one night and in the same service was healed of a bleeding ulcer in his stomach. Another gentleman in her church had a brain tumor that secular doctors refused to operate on. He was miraculously led to a Christian doctor, unknown to anyone in the congregation, who counseled him to come to his hospital. This particular doctor, who trusted in Christ, prayed that the Lord would lead him in the operation, and by God's grace and power the operation saved the man's life. The man with the tumor was poor and had no money to pay the bill, but by the time the man went into surgery, the exact amount of money needed was miraculously provided. Linda Tobman wrote the following:

"What is a Missionary? A person willing to go when the call of the Lord comes, willing to do what ever the Lord asks one to do, at any time of day or night, and any kind of work. One must have compassion, not bad judgment; one must see the soul crying out for help; and realizing that if you do not take the truth to them, that person will enter hell for an eternity. Isaiah 6:8 says: 'Whom shall I send, and who will go for us?' I was forty-nine when I first went on the mission field. My only experience for qualifying was being a wife, mother, Sunday school teacher and being a

Bible School graduate. Eagerly I went where the Holy Ghost was sending me."

Through many obstacles and trials, including devastating earthquakes and major mudslides in the mountains where she resides, Linda Tobman continues to reach the people that God has sent her to. May the Lord continue to bless this worthy missionary and her ministry.

Rev. Dr. William F. Hill:
Missionary-Pastor (written by Rev. William F. Hill and Debra Stacey)

William F. Hill pioneered the Calvary Evangelistic Center in Independence, Iowa in 1965, and has pastored there for over 40 years. In 1975 he founded the Independence Christian Academy, grades K-12, which is now celebrating its 30th year. He has also written twenty-two books and over twenty religious pamphlets. In addition to preaching at camp-meetings, conducting seminars and revival meetings in the USA, God has moved on Dr. Hill to expand the ministry of their local church into all the world through literature and many overseas trips where he has conducted city-wide crusades and seminars. He has received his Th.B., Th.M., and Doctor of Theology degrees from International Seminary, Plymouth, Florida.

Because some of my writings reached believers in Kenya, I received an invitation to Kenya to visit the Kenya Evangelism Team and Crusades.

We went to Kenya and Uganda, East Africa on a three week trip in January, 1983. The culture shock when we drove out of Nairobi was severe. Just a few miles out of the capitol city, we saw giraffes standing along the highway, eating from the trees. Also, we saw a great number of zebras along the road.

Our first night after leaving Nairobi was spent, as many of our nights were, in mud houses, with grass roofs, dirt floors, with no water or electricity.

It seemed God was both merciful and mischievous in that our first night in the African bush was by far the worst I have ever experienced. As the leader of our group I was afforded the honor of having my own private hut. The cot was not that uncomfortable. A mosquito net was draped over me. My luggage sat open on a stool next to where I was to sleep, but sleep, I did not. No, not one minute. A bat circled me all night, while a rat ran up and down the wall next to me, desperately wanting to get into my luggage.

Surely someone would hear my loud cries to scare away the rat, and the bat, but alas, no one heard me to come to my rescue. Believe me, I was ready for the long drive back to Nairobi, to get aboard another jumbo jet for the U.S.A., but it was not to be. From that first night on, the journey to Kenya and Uganda got better.

God gave us many souls and many new friends. We had been told we would fall in love with the Kenyan people, and that we did. Also, we loved the Ugandan people. Our short trek into Uganda was made shortly after the collapse of the dictatorship of the Idi Amin regime. We were stopped every few miles by soldiers of the new Marxist government, wanting to know why we were in their country.

It soon became obvious that we were the only white people from the Kenyan border to the City of Jinja, Uganda. Automatic weapons were constantly pointed at us, even prodding through the open windows of our automobile. One soldier stuck his automatic rifle in our window, and with almost a snarl demanded to know why we were in Uganda.

When I told him we were missionaries, he demanded me to produce gospel tracts. I gave him some. He then demanded I hand him more. When we gave him a large quantity, he broke into a large, friendly smile, shook my hand and said, "Praise God, Brother, I will give one of these to everyone I stop." Upon our second trip to Kenya we were taken to a large slum area in Nairobi. We were warned we must leave before the sun set or our lives would be in great danger.

After the house service was over, we loaded up in the van, knowing we were up against the deadline of the setting of the sun.

The dirt streets were very narrow and our driver, turning a corner, knocked over a man's charcoal cooking stove. The man began screaming at us and a crowd of people came running at the van until we were surrounded. We had the feeling we were in extreme danger as we had been told that even armed soldiers would not enter this massive slum except in groups. Suddenly, a very tall African man came upon the scene and demanded to know what was wrong. When we explained what had happened, he turned on the mob and demanded they move back and allow us to go through. Immediately they fell back.

About two streets later our van dropped into a large mud hole, and we were stuck. This same mob came running up, but now they seemed to be our friends and pushed our van backwards out of the muddy place.

Our driver panicked and backed over someone's goat. It was unbelievable, but God got us out of that area just as the sun was going down. We sent the money to build a church in that large slum area. When we were asked to come back and dedicate that church we decided to let our African brothers have the honor.

In these past 23 years we have had the joy of seeing thousands saved and many churches built. My wife and I were honored to have dinner in the summer palace of a regional king in Nigeria, West Africa, and then to have him come to hear me preach the next day at a large meeting. When I gave him some of my books, he let me know that he had already read some of them. He said he was a Muslim, but now had accepted Jesus Christ. We had such a delightful visit and meal with this king, and his wife and daughter. Just a few months ago when going through security clearance at the Murtala Muhammed International Airport at Lagos, Nigeria, we had another blessed experience. My wife and I had gone through security and were waiting for our fellow minister, Rev. Gary Hampton.

When the security team noticed a large number of books in the carry-on luggage of Gary Hampton, one of the officers asked him for a copy. Rev. Hampton pointed at me and told them that I was the author. (Actually, I co-authored the book with Evangelist J. A. Ajeigbe, Ilesa, Nigeria.) One of the officers brought me back to the x-ray machines, gave me his chair, and asked me to inscribe the names of the other security officers along with my signature. And so, for about the next twenty minutes I sat there and signed books for this elite group of airport security officers.

God has blessed the books He has helped me to write. They have gone literally around the world. Some of my books have been translated and printed now in English, Spanish, French, Arabic, Hebrew, Burmese, Urdu, Russian and Chinese, plus local languages. Of course, God deserves all of the praise and glory for this. An outstanding event took place about twenty years ago in Freetown, Sierra Leone, West Africa. We had about 750 converts in five nights of meetings. One of these converts, a Muslim, asked me to baptize him in water the following Sunday. He was one of only two people I have baptized in a foreign country.

In 2005 we were preaching and teaching in a very large seminar in Nigeria, where thousands were attending. An African man walked up to me and said, "Do you remember me?" I asked him to give me a hint, or clue. He said, "You baptized me in water after your crusade in Freetown, Sierra Leone." I immediately said to him, "You are Simeon Kamara." He informed me that he now has his own ministry in Monrovia, Liberia. He said he wanted me to know that the fruit of that meeting so many years ago, was still living on. Think about it! Saved in Sierra Leone, meets me in Nigeria, and tells me of his ministry in Liberia. A few weeks ago I accepted his invitation and my wife, Betty, and I spent a few weeks with him in Monrovia. He has raised up a strong church, and has seven preachers he is training to raise up churches in Liberia.

I taught a Pastor's seminar for three hours each morning and conducted an Evangelistic Crusade each evening. Many were saved, some were filled with the Holy Spirit, and others were healed.

It was such an honor to stand beside Simeon Kamara in an African river just a few blocks from the Atlantic Ocean, assisting in baptizing 35 people from his Church who had qualified for water baptism.

Three of those we baptized were Muslims who had recently converted to Christ from Islam. One had even made his pilgrimage to Mecca, one of the holiest shrines of Islam.

From Monrovia, Liberia, we flew to Freetown, Sierra Leone, for a Pastor's Seminar and Evangelistic Crusade with Pastor Bockarie Mansaray who has raised up a church of hundreds. Against unbelievable odds he has also raised up the Elim International Christian Academy with 337 students enrolled from grades 1-6. Some of the students are from Muslim families who would rather have their children taught Christianity than send them to the public schools. Yes, God's world-wide missionary work is so exciting!

Dr. Hill baptizing souls in Liberia

Visiting a Bible College in Myanmar

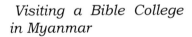

Dr. Hill at a Myanmar Bible College

Gene Thompson: (went to be with the Lord recently) *Missionary to Ukraine & Siberia*

Several Ukrainians with Gene Thompson & John Duncan

THE MIRACLE OF FAITH MISSION

The history of Faith Mission started in 1987. After hearing the plight of the people living behind the Iron Curtain, the Lord placed a burden upon my heart. Two years later, in 1989, the door opened for a visit to Bulgaria. While in this country, which was still a police state, the burden became greater as I saw the needs of the people and their hunger for God. In 1991, the door opened for me to go into the country of Ukraine which was the third largest of the Soviet Union countries.

In October 1991, my brother, Wilburn Thompson, and I (who are from central Florida) received an invitation to visit Ukraine. This was one and a half months after the fall of the Communist government. It was on this first visit of 17 days that the Lord began to formulate the work of Faith Mission.

We had no knowledge of the "underground" church in the Soviet Union when we went to Ukraine. It was by divine providence that we met the leader of the Pentecostal "underground" churches that was the "persecuted" church of Russia. This system of churches, over 1,500 groups, was under the leadership of Ivan Levchuk. Brother Levchuk had suffered 25 years in prison for his belief in God. We were introduced to many of the pastors of these cell groups and told of their suffering for the Gospel. For 72 years Russia had controlled all of the surrounding countries with an atheistic government denying them knowledge of God.

Faith Mission began as a full time ministry in 1992. We were able to register our mission work with the new Ukrainian government. This opened many doors. Because of the Soviet system that had controlled everything, there were many difficulties. Our work began by visiting the "house churches." The unregistered believers were not allowed to have a church building. Later, we were allowed to go use the former culture halls, go into the schools, and have street services. There was a great harvest of souls from these meetings. We built our first church in 1993 in the city of Zhitomir, Ukraine. From this church, we have gone out into surrounding villages with the Gospel, which most of the people have never heard. In these villages, we have started new churches and built places of worship where there was no church of any kind for as many as 400 years.

Congregation of Zhitomir, Ukraine Church

The ministry of Faith Mission moved into Promorskiy Krai, the Far East of Russia, where a church was built in 1993. In 2002, the Lord again caused the ministry of Faith Mission to grow through a burden for the need in Siberia. Truly God worked His will and the mystery of His power in opening the Siberian work. In July 2002, God began to deal with our heart about this need. Just as in Ukraine, when we had no knowledge of an underground church, we had no knowledge of anyone in Siberia. We began to follow the leading of the Spirit, and the destination was Yagodnoe, Siberia. This is the area where Stalin had the Gulag prison camps and where many of the Christians suffered and died.

Church building in Piski

In Yagodnoe, Siberia, we found a native man and his wife that had been filled with the Holy Ghost. Together they had been praying for five years asking God to give them a church. God heard their prayer. While flying over Europe in July 2002, on a return trip home from Ukraine, God spoke to my heart. In just over one and a half years, we had a "miracle" church in Siberia. It is certainly a "miracle" because the building was a former Orthodox church. The Orthodox does not accept Protestants and other religious groups, but fights against them. By God's divine providence, the local priest sold us the building. There is now a Pentecostal church in Yagodnoe, Siberia. There are no churches for hundreds of miles in the Kolyma region of Siberia where Yagodnoe is located.

JAMES MARTIN - from Texas
(works with the Native Americans tribes)

After nearly two decades of pastoral ministry, God has chosen us to step out in faith to offer "Hope for the Home" through a ministry to local churches as God opens the doors under the blessing of concerned pastors. With this vision, our family ministers in songs, Scripture passage quotations, and messages that focus on applying biblical values in the power of the Spirit to the vital relationships in our lives.

Included in God's call to "Hope for the Home" is a dimension of home missions to the Native Americans (sometimes called American Indians). One missions report stated that the Native Americans are one of the neediest of unreached people groups in the world. Only about 2% of Native Americans claim to be Christians. And this is after more than 300 years of missionary activity. The bondage of bitterness, alcohol and drug abuse, and idolatrous religion touches the heart of God. We do not have the authority to give them back their land; however, we do have an anointing to give them Jesus who heals the brokenhearted and sets the captives free.

James Douglas Martin was born July 24, 1960 to Rev. Harley and Christene Martin in Fort Worth, Texas. He had the distinct privilege of being raised in a godly environment where the Word of God and prayer had a dominant place in the home. His fondest memory of his childhood was being snuggled under his dad's arm at the green rocking chair during family devotions, and hearing his dad call his name in prayer. From a young and tender age, he knew that God's hand was upon him. He experienced a Samuel-like calling when he was about 12 years old. After many nights of deep troubling, and prayer meetings with his parents, he heard the voice of the Lord saying, "Whom shall I send, and who will go for us?" He responded with a trembling, but whole-hearted willingness, and was assured of God's calling to preach. After this time, he was subjected to aptitude tests in the public school which he attended. He told the teacher, "I do not know what career your test will show that I should pursue, but I know that God wants me to be a preacher."

James's parents ensured that he had good, wholesome books to read. He was deeply impacted by the biography of 'Praying Hyde.' It challenged him to a disciplined prayer life, rising early to spend time with the Lord before going to school.

His fellow students recognized God's call upon his life, and the Student Council asked him to give a devotional each morning over the PA system for the high school with 2000 students where he attended.

On July 10, 1977 James was praying at the altar of the church where his dad was the pastor. Everyone else had already risen from prayer, and were fellowshipping with each other. He felt a strong hand upon his shoulder, and glanced around to see who was praying for him. There was no one there! The presence of the Lord engulfed him, and he felt a distinct calling to be a missionary.

After graduation, James prayerfully considered further preparation for ministry. His home church sponsored a mission trip to the Apache Indian Reservation in Cedar Creek, Arizona. On July 20, 1978 he was invited to attend the funeral of a backslidden Apache woman. He was stirred by the peculiarities of the ceremony: the last of the wailing relatives placed an open package of cheese and crackers as well as an open Sprite drink in the casket beside the dead woman's head. After lowering the casket into the ground, they placed all of her belongings in the grave as well. At the mission church service that night, the Spirit of God spoke forcibly in his spirit: "I want you to be a missionary to these people in your own home country. They must have more than cheese and crackers – they need the Bread of Life. They must have more than Sprite, and certainly more than "fire water" – they need the Water of Life. And they must get it before they die!" From that time there was no question about the direction of his life and ministry.

James was influenced by David & Donna Tucker to consider Ozark Bible Institute (OBI) in Neosho, Missouri as the place to pursue his educational and spiritual preparation for ministry. During his first year there, on February 2, 1979, one of the instructors spoke of the Constraint of the Call. He made comment of the fact that we are sometimes naturally inclined to want to visit certain places, and would consider it a thrill to be called to minister there. But there are other places of hardship to which one would not be drawn to, "such as Alaska". It hit his heart like a bomb! Would he be willing to even go to Alaska to preach the Gospel to the native people? He was gripped so mightily by the Spirit's call that he would never forget the agonizing prayer of submission that followed.

God knew the importance of providing a competent help meet for James. On May 31, 1980, James was married to Carol Lea Noland, whom he met at OBI. She was the daughter of Rev. Jimmy & Murlene Noland from Arkansas. An interesting aspect of their meeting and marriage is the fact that they were both born on July 24, 1960. According to the birth certificates, Carol was born one minute before James. She was born in St. Mary's Hospital in Russellville, AR and he was born in St. Joseph's Hospital in Fort Worth, TX -- there you have Mary and Joseph together! Both of their dads were Pentecostal pastors. It was not just a coincidence!

After completing four years at OBI, they served as Assistant Pastors in Texarkana, TX. Then they pastored in Conway, AR and Mount Vernon, TX for a combined total of 17 years. They strove to be faithful, and learned many valuable lessons through practical experience. These years were of tremendous value in preparation for the extensive ministry for which God was preparing them.

God favored their marriage with ten children, five boys and five girls. At one point, James was fervently praying about some special needs in the lives of one of his children. He felt so completely inadequate to provide the needed training. He sought the Lord, and he received a scripture and promise from the Lord. He was directed to Romans 15:13, "And the God of hope fill you with all joy and peace in believing, that ye may abound in hope through the power of the Holy Ghost." God spoke to him, "There is hope for your home in the Lord."

God assured him that what He would give him answers for his home, and that he would someday have the opportunity to share those truths with others. That was the beginning of Hope for the Home Ministries.

In the fall of the year 2000, they resigned their pastorate, and began full-time missionary/evangelistic ministry. Their first direct contact with Indians came near Choctaw, Oklahoma while they were preaching a revival for Pastor Paul & Jane Nix.

Pastor Nix accompanied James to visit the Kickapoo tribal offices, but since no one except for a secretary was available, they were instructed to talk with a Wycliffe Bible translator who was working with their language. He told them how hard it was to be accepted with the Kickapoo. He had  been with them, both in Oklahoma and Mexico, for 13 years, and was only now beginning to see signs of acceptance. It was obvious that God's favor must open the hearts. At the service that night, fervent prayer was made that God would indeed grant favor and open doors.

The next day, they drove down the road marked "No Trespassing" into the area where the Kickapoo homes were on the banks of the South Canadian River. They stopped where several women, a man, and some children were in the yard between two houses.

Native Americans & Rev. Martin

The short, square-shouldered, 70 year old man came forward, and asked tersely, "What do you want?" Pastor Nix replied, "Do you remember a man who brought firewood to you last year? He attends my church." The man replied, "Yes, I remember. That was a great help to us." James saw right there how that good works prepare the way for the Gospel. James introduced himself to the man, Johnny Chakenatho, and asked his forgiveness for the way that the white man had mistreated the Indians. Large tears welled up in Johnny's eyes as he accepted the humble apology. He began to reminisce about many incidents of racial prejudice that were so hurtful to him. James discovered that the two women also outside were significant leaders in working with the children of the tribe. When they were asked in what ways they needed help, they requested children's clothes and car seats. James assured them that he would do all he could to help them. Within about 30 minutes, he invited James and Pastor Nix into his home, where he displayed his art work and arrowhead collection. Thus began a continuing friendship with Johnny and the Kickapoo people. Since then Hope for the Home Ministries has delivered many boxes of clothes, toys, and gifts to the Kickapoo people in Oklahoma and Eagle Pass, TX.

Gail Myers:
(Mexico, Panama, and Columbia)

A Brief History of Gail Myers: (adapted from an article found in The Holiness Informer, 2004 Winter edition) "The following article gives a brief overview of the great work done by Sis. Gail Myers. It was written a few years ago, so it goes without saying even more has been accomplished since then." – Bryan Gish

"The missionary work of Holiness Full Gospel Missions began close to (50 years) ago in Mexico. Gail Myers was led by the Holy Ghost to make a decision to dedicate her life to the work in Mexico. No one invited her to visit in Mexico, as is the custom today. She made the choice to work for God and sell out, then resigned her position with the U.S. Government in Fort Knox, Kentucky and left for the mission field.

Twenty-five years ago, Gail Myers went to Panama to the Kuna Indians on the San Blas Islands and in the jungle. Today the work extends into Panama proper to the Kunas and Panamanians. Praise and thanksgiving belong to the Lord for the support of the Holiness churches in America, for their faith in the work and their prayers. The Holiness churches in America are "share-holders" in the work, and share in every soul that is saved.

More than 140 churches have been built in Mexico and 25 in Panama. Most of the churches in Panama were built in the San Blas Islands for the Kuna Indians, and some for the Panamanians. For 25 years, radio broadcasts have reached all parts of Mexico and many Latin American nations. At least 15 Latin American countries have been heard from as a result.

Gail Myers traveling through Ole' Mexico

Those that hear the broadcast write of hunger and happiness to be able to receive the Holiness message by means of radio. There are two programs each week, one directed into Mexico and the other to the West Indies Islands of the Caribbean Sea. For Holiness Full Gospel Missions, the radio broadcast is one of the greatest outreaches. They hear and see many results from the radio ministry.

Bible training schools have also been started. About 35 years ago a training center was begun in Victoria, Mexico and later one began in Jimenez, Mexico, which has been operating for over 25 years. These schools were part of the dream and vision of Sister Gail. At least 200 students have gone out of the training centers, making some of the best and most faithful ministers. Many of them hold positions of responsibility and are wonderful leaders in the work of Holiness Full Gospel Missions. What a blessing this has been to Mexico, for these men came from a background of Roman Catholicism and little or no education. Plans are being made to begin two new training schools in 1997: one in the San Blas Islands, and one in Panama proper.

The warehouse, mission home and official office of Holiness Full Gospel Missions is in Edinburg, Texas. There much work is carried out for the Lord: office work, plus the receiving of clothes, beans, rice, etc. into the warehouse. It is from this official headquarters that ministers and their helpers are received to carry items into Mexico for those in need. All correspondence and financial reports go out from this office as well.

Gail Myers is the founder of Holiness Full Gospel Missions in Mexico and Panama. She has been the president and administrator through all the years of the mission's existence, and God has greatly anointed her to carry the Gospel to the lost of these needy nations.

Shirley Savage:
(Short-Term Missionary trip to Panama)

Always Ready For Anything
By: Shirley Savage

In 1996, Gail Myers called and asked if I would go with her to Panama. Oh, I was so excited. Little did I realize the joy I would receive on that trip. On October 14, 1996, at 4:17 a.m. we left the house and headed for the airport. At 6:30 p.m. we arrived in Panama city. Our group included Jim Suits, Rick Binkley, Darrel Hosman, Gail Myers and myself. Natives, Frankie and his wife Ameda also went with us.

We arose at 3:15 a.m. Wednesday morning and boarded a small plane. This was more than a routine for Gail Myers, this was her life. She wanted every church visited, with no one left out. We landed in Playon, Chico. After landing on a strip the size of a driveway we helped unload the plane. Then, like follow-the-leader, we walked through bushes to the other side of the island where we were greeted by the Kuna Indians. There we climbed into our canoe. I watched as Gail Myers climbed in and out of two canoes, in and out of the small planes, and walked through the brush—never complaining; just walking and talking.

As our canoes were approaching Mami Tapo we could see the smiles on the faces and hear the people calling out, "Mama Gail!, Mama Gail!" It felt as though you were riding with the President of the United States! You could see and feel the love these people had for Gail Myers. We were on this island for three days, holding a convention. The Lord blessed each service in a great way.

Gail Myers sees that each pastor on the islands have an apartment size cook stove. This way, they were able make and sell bread to help their income.

She and I shared a hut and each of us slept in a hammock. There was no electricity, only our flashlight. The first night on the island in our hut I came to realize we were not alone. Running over the rafters were white and black rats—huge! Most were over a foot long!! Some time during the night, I was awakened by her saying, "Get off me, mister! You do not belong here." I turned my flashlight toward her and there was a big white rat running away—off of her shoulder! She just smiled and said, "Now, we can go to sleep." That wasn't all—someone had tied a rooster to our hut. We never slept.

There were 125 huts on this island and 1,400 people. So, you can imagine how close the huts are to each other. We had prayer meetings at 4:00 a.m. each morning. Gail Myers was always ready and eager to do something for God, and for the people.

Later, we went to I Dee Dee Gonda. On one of the islands, the pastor and his wife were building a church. They did not have a cement mixer so the pastor's wife mixed the cement with her feet. Her feet had cracked and gotten infected. She came to Gail Myers and showed them to her. She took those dirty, infected feet in her hands and she prayed. She gave this lady something to wash her feet with and some salve to put on them. I watched, in awe, as she not only taught the Word, but taught practical things as well.

After visiting and having services on the islands we returned to Panama City. There, I asked Gail Myers how to use the phone to call home. She looked so sad as she said, "I do not know. I have never called the states from here. I do not have anyone to call." My heart broke! This woman has no family—how alone!

As we lay in our hammocks at night she would talk and talk. One night I fell asleep while she was talking. When I awoke she said, "I am so sorry! You see, I do not have anyone to talk to in English. I even dream in Spanish." On another night I asked her, "What is your secret in the Ministry?" She replied, "It is no secret. I just make myself available."

One sight I will never forget was that of leaving each island—men, women, and children would follow Gail Myers as far as they could. Tears would be streaming down their faces as they were waving and calling out, "Bye, Mama Gail! We love you!"

And one day it will be "Bye", for the last time, to this Great Lady of God who never had children of her own blood, but who had hundreds of children—all around the world.

Rev. Curtis Teague & family

African
Holiness Missions:

How We Started:

The holiness work in the country of Cameroon was birthed in the heart of Rev. Curtis Teague during his first trip to this Western African nation. When he arrived and saw first hand what

the Lord was doing in that place, he knew that he was supposed to be a part of it. "When I arrived there, I was greeted by hungry souls eager to hear from the Word of the Lord. I found a people living in huts made from mud and thatch, with no electricity or running water. A people bound by superstition and witchcraft. A people who readily received the message of hope Christ gives". Since that time, he and other ministry partners have made many trips to

Cameroon, with great numbers coming out of the darkness and into the marvelous Light.

Where We Are Going:

Currently we have over 20 churches that are a part of African Holiness Missions. These are churches that either we or our converts have planted. We have churches among the Pygmy in the rain forest and among the Muslim saturated Northern provinces, with a good representation all across the country. Currently, there are just under 1000 people making up the congregations of these twenty eight churches. We have a Cameroon native full time missionary that we support on a monthly basis to be our field representative. We also have a board of directors that have proven to be a great blessing to our work in Africa. They are as follows; Curtis Teague, chairman; Kenneth Lott, vice chairman; Timothy Hudson, secretary/ treasurer; Cecil Buchannon; and Ryan Ralston.

Testimony of **Delphine:**
written by Rev. Teague

This woman is from the extreme Northern town of Maga.

She is a member of Pastor Raymond Souboursous' congregation. Her story is one unlike any that I have ever heard, a story of great faith, courage, and confidence in God. Several years ago, she came to a Christian service looking for answers in her life. When the preacher told the story of Jesus, the Holy Ghost convicted the heart of Delphine. She made her way to the altar during the invitation and gave her life to Christ. The story sounds very familiar up to this point, but Delphine knew that her coming forward in this service and giving her life to the Lord would have severe consequences. Her husband is a Muslim and practices the religion of Islam. For her to make a break from that and come to Christ would indeed cost her dearly. After many beatings and endless abuse, both physically and mentally, he gave her the ultimatum. Leave Jesus and your church, or get out of my house and take the children you have born to me with you. She chose Jesus! It is not easy for a woman with three children to make it in a place like Maga without the support of a husband, but by the grace of God and the help of His people, she has and will make it. Please pray for sister Delphine and the children, and by all means pray for her husband that God would reach him with the power of the gospel.

The Sumner family: Missionaries to Honduras
(written by Alan Sumner)

Rev. Jake and Brenda Sumner of Tulsa, OK., and their two sons, eight year-old Alan and five year-old Scott Sumner started Christ Cares World Ministries about forty years ago. After graduating from Bible College, the Sumners made their first missionary trip to the Central American nation of Nicaragua where they witnessed the beginning of their first church, and God began what would become a lifetime of ministry to the Spanish speaking peoples of Latin America.

As missionary-evangelists the Sumner family has traveled full-time, living in motorhomes, travel trailers, buses and even boats when necessary. They have ministered in every country in Central America as well as extensively in Belize, and Mexico. The works they started continue to prosper by the grace of God.

In January 1990, Jake, Brenda, Alan, (with his new bride Paula), Scott (with his wife of one year, Bonita), began what would become the longest stay in any single country and the most ambitious effort since Christ Cares' founding. What was initially an effort that ministered to thousands of refugees in three different encampments led to a ministry effort among the Nicaraguan Contra fighters. This in turn opened the door for them to preach to the Honduran Military and Police force.

What started slowly and with some resistance to "Evangelical Gringos" preaching on Military bases has grown to an acceptance and confidence where Military commanders, Officers and enlisted men and women regularly call for prayer and spiritual guidance. With over 19 years as the unofficial Military and Police chaplains they are literally preaching and ministering from coast to coast to thousands on a regular scheduled basis. They preach in every academy in the country; Army, Navy, Air Force and the Police academies.

They regularly preach to all Police candidates in the two Centers for Police Instruction (C.I.P.). Literally, all Police, Military personal and facilities are open to them.
Traveling by land, sea and air they are visiting some of the most remote and neglected regions of the country such as the 'mosquitia jungle'. In the city of Danlí, the Christ Cares Church is a beach-head for the holiness message in a land where liberalism and the Charismatic message is the norm. With well over 100 in regular attendance, God has given the Sumners a good group of hungry hearts who desire a true sanctified life. From these sincere and dedicated servants, God has raised up workers who are now being involved in many outreaches through the local church, such as Hospital, Prison, Street and Door-To-Door evangelism are some examples of what they are involved in.

As of 2009, there are twelve members in the missionary family; Jake, Brenda, Alan, Paula (with their three daughters), Rachel, Ruth, Rhoda, Scott, Bonita (with their three daughters), Hannah, Elizabeth and Sarah. All twelve are actively involved in this ministry outreach in Sunday School, Children's and Youth Ministries, Children's Saturday School and even a soup kitchen where children receive not only a nourishing meal but hear the precious Words that give Eternal Life.

Honduras "Water Baptismal Service"

As they approach the twenty year mark of ministering in Honduras, they look forward to the many more doors that God will open. They are excited about the souls that will come to Christ and they pray that God would send young couples with a burning desire to see God move in these last days in this region of the world.

Joseph Barraclough:
Vision Ministries International

Vision Ministries International (VMI) is the missionary ministry of the Barraclough Family, comprised of Joe & Judith Barraclough and their four children, Nadia, Isaac, Jennifer, & Caleb. VMI is an outreach of Global Missionary Taskforce, Inc., (GMT) a missionary-sending agency of which Joe is the co-founder and Secretary/Treasurer.

A Brief History

Joe began preaching at the age of sixteen, three years after his conversion. God began dealing with him about missions work when he was still a teenager. As the years passed, Joe continued in pastoral ministry, waiting upon the Lord for direction concerning his call to missions. During this time, God gave him a dream. In the dream, he was standing beside tribal Indians in the rainforest, conversing with them in Spanish. Coupled with a burden for the Latin American peoples, the dream confirmed to him that he was called to minister in Latin America, and would some day work in pioneer jungle ministry. From this time, he worked to learn Spanish, and also studied the various countries and people groups of South America.

Joe married at the age of 23 to Judith (Fonseca), and the young couple continued in various areas of pastoral ministry. Five years later, upon the invitation of veteran missionary Chuck Akers, Jr., the family moved to Venezuela, South America to begin their career as full-time missionaries. While in Venezuela, the Barraclough family worked in pastoral ministry, youth outreach, children's ministry, street evangelism and music ministry in the slums of the capital city, Caracas.

The family looked forward to ministering in this nation for many years; however, a medical emergency whisked the family backed to the States in early 2005 when their fifth child, Melissa Faith, passed away. With the political tension growing in that nation and receiving direction from the Lord, the family knew it was time to leave Venezuela. They departed the country in April 2006.

After their departure from Venezuela, the family labored in co-pioneering a church-planting ministry among an unreached people group, the Naso Indians of northwestern Panama. God continues to work among the Naso Indians, and the ministry is maturing under national leadership through the efforts of several GMT missionaries.

At present, Joe is working to open up new works in Latin America through pioneer evangelism, children's crusades, revival campaigns and pastoral conferences. They are presently focusing on the nation of Perú, South America. In addition to his work as a field missionary, Joe also provides accounting services to all GMT missionaries, oversees the administration of GMT, is active in the training of first-term foreign missionaries affiliated with GMT, and as opportunity affords, is a visiting instructor at

Ozark Bible Institute & College, teaching missions-related classes.

Our Vision:
It is the thrust of Vision Ministries to establish indigenous works among unreached and less-reached people groups in Latin America and equip national pastors with the ministerial skills necessary to enable them to fulfill their vision.

A Remarkable Testimony of Provision:
As mentioned earlier, Joe had felt the call to foreign missions in his youth; however it would be approximately ten years before he would launch out into missionary work. The following tells how God's plan for him unfolded.

While working for as a Chief Financial Officer for a secular employer, God spoke to Joe Barraclough about going full time into missions work in about six months time. Full of faith and knowing he was walking in the center of God's will, Joe arrived at work the next day, stepped into the office of his boss and, mustering all the courage he had, directly told his boss that the time had come for him to begin full-time missions work. Before Joe was able to offer to remain at the job for six more months, to train his replacement, his boss told him, "If this is the way you feel, and you are no longer committed to this company, go clean out your desk and go home; you are fired!"

Perplexed by his boss's response and being immediately released from his job, he brought his question to the Lord: Was he not supposed to continue at that job for six more months? The Lord never responded to his petition that day; however, later that evening, his boss called him, and apologized for his abrupt behavior that morning. In the ensuing conversation, he asked him to stay on at the job for six more months and train his replacement. To this he readily agreed, knowing this was indeed God's will. What was so puzzling that day had now become a confirmation of being in God's perfect timing.

In those final six months the Barracloughs set their hearts on the mission field. They paid off their remaining debts, worked and prayed hard to "trust" God, and began to notify churches and friends of their career change.

Seven churches pledged to financially support the family by the end of those six months, but when the family was ready to make the big step to go to Venezuela, little money had come in.

After settling their financial debts, Joe had just enough money remaining to rent a moving van and purchase airplane tickets to Caracas, Venezuela. They planned to move their belongings from Arizona to Texas, and board a plane for Venezuela, knowing that this would consume all their resources. The lack of finances however did not deter the family for proceeding with their plans. They knew beyond the shadow of a doubt that God was leading them.

Finally, the last day at his job for Joe came. After shaking hands with his boss to say good-bye, while halfway to the door, his boss called out to him. As he turned around, his boss casually said, "Here is something to help you get started in missions work." He reached out and accepted a check from his boss; it was in the amount of $10,000! As always, God supplied the need right on time!

This initial miraculous provision for their missions work became the first of many as this devoted family stepped into the perfect will of God, confirming Hudson Taylor's old adage, "God's work done in God's way, will never lack God's supply." The man who fired Joe six months earlier, was the very one moved on by God to be the instrument of supplying their financial need!

Baptizing a Panamanian boy (above); Preaching in Panama (below)

Harold Bruce: (Pastor and Missionary)

Raised in the home of a pastor I was afforded the early introduction of missions into my life. I remember as a mere boy of 10 years old how I would sit on the floor in the living room and listen to the eminent world evangelist Bill Burkett talk of the saints in Russia, the ways of the church, and the perils of his journey. My imagination was enraptured but something more important was going on in the heart of a little boy, a spark had ignited the flame of world evangelism. It would be 23 years before I would take my first mission trip, and though just a meager preacher from a small church in Ohio, I had the privilege to minister on four continents in 2008 alone!

I believe every committed mission worker, and every dedicated world evangelist can point to that day or event when the spark of the Holy Ghost ignited the passion that burns for the lost. Many preachers can point to the person whom God used to spark that flame of consuming desire to preach in all the world. This spark of faith that separates those who stay from those who "go", this spark of faith that turns Jerusalem preachers into utter most preachers is imparted by anointed men of God; I have found Dr. Pahlman to be one of these select men. He has yielded his ministry to the endeavor of igniting a generation to go into all the world. Fanning the flame of world evangelism, the SENT Ministries is setting on fire a generation that is inspired, equipped, and led into the Harvest Field. The "hands on" approach of short term missions is life changing for the evangelist, pastor and church worker and has a direct impact on the Kingdom of God. The consistency of the SENT program is a testimony of the consuming nature of the true call of God in Dr. Pahlman's life, one given to the supreme belief in God's word that we must go, that we must plant the seed of desire in others to go.

As we look on the Harvest and the billions of souls to be won to the cause of Christ it gives me great joy and encouragement knowing we have a fellow laborer and friend in Pastor Pahlman, filled with the Holy Ghost and fire;

SENT by God, SENT to this generation, and SENT into all the world!

Pastor Bruce ministering in Africa

Rev. Matt Jones Broadway Assembly, Lorain, Ohio

"Called To Reach"-

The Great Commission was the last major command given by Christ to the church. It was His order for us to march, and it was non-negotiable. His expectation was that we busy ourselves with the task of reaching and teaching both locally and globally.

For approximately eight years, our church in Lorain has joined with two other congregations in northeast Ohio, Calvary Pentecostal Tabernacle of Wooster (Pastor Dan Brimm) and Central Assembly of Mentor (Pastor Charles Pahlman), to revitalize our global mission to reach beyond our communities. We scheduled a weekend to spotlight our missions vision by holding a conference in which three missionaries would come to share their vision and work with our churches. We planned and pursued that date with excitement, and I can say that we have never regretted that decision, for we have reaped the benefits annually.

We have raised our awareness of the call to global missions in the following ways:

1.   Youth have come forward to accept the call to ministry and have taken steps to pursue it.

2.   We have increased our prayer support for global missionaries.

3.   We have increased our financial support for global missions.

We three pastors readily acknowledge that our Northeast Ohio Missions Conference has revolutionized our churches' global vision, and I look forward to continuing this worthwhile effort with these fellowshipping brethren. I appreciate hearing of other Missions conventions being conducted in our church movement and encourage pastors and congregations to get involved in having a yearly meeting of their own if they have not yet done so. I am convinced that they will never regret the decision to promote the greatest work in the world- The Great Commission of Christ!

N.E. Ohio Global Missions Convention 2007

Missionaries:(l-r: Rev. Joe Barraclough,
Rev. Gene Thompson, Rev. Jerry Back)

Host Pastors: (l-r: Pastor Dan Brimm, Pastor Matt Jones, Pastor Charles Pahlman)

Charles and Denise Pahlman

S.O.N. & S.E.N.T. Ministries

I was born in Cheswick, PA, a suburb of Pittsburgh, in 1961. At the age of twenty-one, I became born again and was then filled with the Holy Ghost.

I attended and graduated from Free Gospel Bible Institute in Export, Pennsylvania(1985-1988). In December of 1988, Denise Lantz and I were married in Goshen, Indiana. We have since been blessed with two precious daughters, Abigail and Elisabeth. Our first pastorate was in Carlisle, Pennsylvania from 1992 to 1998. We then followed the Lord's call to pastor in Mentor, Ohio where we currently serve.

While pastoring in Pennsylvania, I strongly felt the Lord dealing with me to become more actively involved in mission work. Up to this point I had taken two short term missions trips to Lima, Peru and to Mexico. God began to open doors of opportunity, and I took my next mission trip in 1996 to visit Linda Tobman's work in Taiwan. Since that time, I have had the privilege of ministering in 13 different countries including the Philippines, Croatia, Nigeria, Burma, Kenya and India. As of July 2011, I am making plans to minister in Ireland, Germany and Uganda.

While traveling to foreign countries and various people groups, I began to realize the value and priority some cultures place on education. Recognizing that the Lord could use this tool to open doors to further spread the gospel, I began working on my own graduate studies. By God's grace, I earned a Master of Divinity degree in 2002 and a Doctorate of Ministry degree in 2004, both from American Christian College and Seminary in Oklahoma City. I have recently been accepted in the Master's degree program in Leadership Studies at Liberty University.

In 1997, the Lord laid it upon my heart to begin Sprinkle of Nations (S.O.N.) Ministries, a short term missionary endeavor. The name is taken from Isaiah 52:15:

"So shall He sprinkle many nations..." In 2005, by God's grace, I launched S.E.N.T. Ministries, (Student Evangelism to the Nations Teams), taking college age students on short term mission trips in order to encourage them to develop a heart for long term missions.

Eventually the Lord made a way for me to teach as an adjunct faculty member at Free Gospel Bible Institute, teaching *An Introduction to World Missions.* I also taught for three years at Great Lakes Bible Institute in Lorain, Ohio.

With the Lord's help, I have recently developed a five course discipleship program, *The Decorated Disciple,* to help train Christian believers and workers around the world. I have also developed a Christian Leadership program entitled *The Master's Minister.* God has allowed me to use these materials to train ministers, especially in other countries where theological resources are limited.

Teaching in Ilesa, Nigeria

With Dr. Hill in Kale, Myanmar

Traveling on the Old Burma Road

A house Church in Ivanic, Croatia

With the children in Ilesa, Nigeria

Abigail Pahlman in Varazdin, Croatia- 2004

With top Military Chaplains in Sierra Leone - 2009

Granting   Pastor   David Rassily   a   'Decorated Discipleship' Diploma- 2007

Teaching Pastors in S.E. India

Dedicating   a   church   in Bombay India- 2007

SENT Team #1- 2008 Church dedication in Bombay, India

Ministering   in   Ocotlan, Mexico (09).

Standing with Missionary Jeremy Brook

2007 SENT Team preaching in Bombay, India

First SENT Team with Rev. Thomas Peretic in the Philippines- 2005

Discipleship Meeting in Bombay, India

Daughter Abigail & I in Danli, Honduras- 2011

*Abigail Pahlman &
Brittnay Carman
   working with
   children in
   Honduras-
(Jan. 2011)*

*Praying for a Nigerian
King: (2010)*

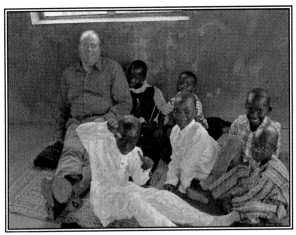

*Resting with
Christian boys of
Abeokuta, Nigeria
(2010)*

During the Nigerian SENT program- 2010

Preaching in Oyo State, Nigeria (2010)
with interpreter Rev. Laney

*Standing at the entrance of Adoniram Judson's
Memorial Church: Yangon, Myanmar (Burma)-2004}*

June 2011: Ministering in Webuye, Kenya with Dr. Wm. Hill, Rev. Mike Johnson. Kenyan leader Rev. Andrew Wafula (left)

Presenting *The Decorated Disciple* book to a pastor's wife at a Mt. Elgon church in Kenya (2011)

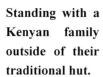

Standing with a Kenyan family outside of their traditional hut.

With Dr. Wm. Hill, praying for people after a Crusade service in Webuye, Kenya (2011)

Standing with Kenyan children on Mt. Elgon, N.W. Kenya

Conclusion

Close to half a century ago, J. Oswald Smith wrote a book entitled *The Cry of the World*. The name of this missionary work adequately summarizes the spiritual condition of multitudes of people in every nation who know not the Lord!

It is one of my passions to work alongside many other God-loving men and women to help remedy the greatest problem known to man by bringing the Good News of the Gospel to a lost and dying world. In this book, I have endeavored to clarify the point that we all bear the responsibility to do what we can to fulfill the Great Commission. No one person or group can do the work alone. May the Lord help us, *The Last Days Church*, to cooperate in *reaching the lost at any cost*.

In closing, I wish to encourage and challenge all of my Christian readers with this portion of a devotional by J. Sidlow Baxter: "Think...of those cities in the 'Regions Beyond,' where thousands, yea millions, are really wanting the truth, but do not know it, and cannot find it. Do I now address some younger person who ought to offer as a messenger to them? Does not the thought of their darkness and futile groping stir you, as Paul was 'stirred' over Athens long ago? Let these lines of Eva Doerksen speak to you:

> *If you had been to heathen lands,*
> *Where weary ones with eager hands*
> *Still plead, yet no one understands,*
> *Would you go back? Would you?*

> *If you had seen them in despair,*
> *Beat on the breast, pull out the hair,*
> *While demon powers filled the air,*
> *Would you go back? Would you?*

> *If you had seen the glorious sight,*
> *When heathen people, long in the night,*
> *Are brought from darkness into the light,*
> *Would you go back? Would you?*

Yet still they wait, a weary throng,
They have waited, some, so very long,
When shall despair be turned to song?
I am going back! Would you?

Do I now address some middle-aged or older person who cannot go out to other lands, but who ought to be praying more, or giving more, or encouraging more, or helping more, toward the evangelizing of those cities and peoples? Oh, let the thought of them stir you into compassionate cooperation with those who actually go out there to tell them!"141

If all of Christ's followers will humbly hearken to this passionate counsel, many in the world will hear and believe in Jesus. His laborers shall then one day hear the precious words of the Master say: "*Well done, thou good and faithful servant...enter thou into the joy of thy Lord.*" Matthew 25:21

---

140 www.thebiblechannel.com; Missions Quotes
141 J. Sidlow Baxter, *Awake My Heart*; Zondervan; 1982; p. 300

Discussion Questions

Chapter One:

1. Give three Bible verses that demonstrate how God wants all people to be saved. (p. 21-24)
2. What verse reveals the Apostle Paul's desire for Christians to know that God is no respecter of persons concerning His offer of salvation? (p. 22)
3. What did Martin Luther call John 3:16? (p. 22)
4. Discuss William M. Tidwell's illustration and how it applies to the substitutionary death of Christ. (p.24)
5. What should motivate us to share the gospel? (p. 24)

Chapter Two:

6. Explain what is meant by the statement- "Preaching alone does not save anyone." (p. 26)
7. Briefly explain the beliefs of Secular Humanism. (p. 26)
8. How does God view "good works" in the matter of earning salvation? (pp. 27-28)
9. What aspects of Christ's work & life were needed to provide salvation for the world of sinners? (p. 29)
10. The simple message of salvation is that the world's need of a Savior has been provided. What is so desperately needed now? Explain your answer. (p. 30)

Chapter Three:

11. What did Mike Stachura mean when he stated: "The mark of a great church is not its seating capacity, but its sending capacity." (p. 36)
12. True or False: "Church is only a place for seeking and worshipping God?" Explain your answer (p. 36)
13. What is meant by the statement: "The work of Christian Missions is a team effort?" (p.38)
14. What five questions should we ask concerning *The Great Commission* verse Mark 16:15? Briefly explain each. (pp. 39-42)
15. Attempt to recite C.T. Studd's famous quote. (p. 42)

Chapter Four:

16. Discuss Maltbie D. Babcock's quote (p. 47)
17. What is meant by the phrase- "This generation must reach this generation." (p. 47)
18. How does James' words; *"...be ye doers of the word, and not hearers only..."* (James 1:22) apply to missions work? (p. 49)
19. What is the purpose of the Baptism of the Spirit? (p. 51)
20. Please discuss the following statement: "A careful study of the major revivals in Church history proves that true revival causes the revitalized Church to become not only pure in its doctrine and lifestyle, but passionate in its duty to the Master by obeying the Great Commission." (p. 52)

Chapter Five:

21. Cite some statistics which prove that the Mormons are dedicated to the cause of their false religion. (p. 61)
22. Please discuss the four questions that Wesley said a Christian should ask in regard to their finances. (p. 65)
23. What are the three points known as the *"3- self's"* of missionary work? Briefly explain each. (pp.66-67)
24. Two books on this subject have been masterfully written by Roland Allen: What are their titles? (p. 66)
25. What is meant by this statement?: "A foreign mission church that receives support for its pastor or its projects should practice accountability to the giver..." (p. 69)

Chapter Six:

26. What is the basic method of worldwide evangelism and missions? Take time to discuss this. (p. 73)
27. What is the difference between a general call and a specific call to Missions? (pp. 77-78)
28. How does C. Gordon Olson define Missions? (p. 78)
29. How does The International Mission Board define a long term missionary? (p. 78)

30. Stephen Ross suggested a list of things that home churches can do to support faithful and dedicated long term missionaries: name at least ten. (pp. 81-82)

Chapter Seven:

31. According to Wesley Duewel, what is the greatest need in Missions work? Explain. (p. 91)
32. Explain what J. Oswald Smith meant when he said: "Intercessory prayer is the Christian's most effective weapon." (p. 92)
33. What kinds of prayers should Christians be praying concerning Missions? (pp. 93-94)
34. List a few of the suggestions given by one missionary organization on how to pray for missions. (pp. 95-96)
35. Cite and discuss the quotes of John Knox, George Whitefield and Henry Martyn. (p 101)

Chapter Eight:

36. What are the sad statistics given in this chapter provided by Jon Macon with the CHENNAI TEACHER TRAINING SCHOOL? (p. 108)
37. Discuss the parable of James Weber. (pp. 108-110)
38. Discuss why education about the needs of the world is important? (p. 111)
39. What is the 10/40 Window? What does it teach us about Missions work? (pp. 114-116)
40. How does Paul's desire expressed in Romans 15:20 reflect *The Great Commission*? (p. 116)

Chapter Nine:

41. List two of the statistics from The Barna Research Group concerning professing Christians sharing their faith. (pp. 121-122)
42. What is *Attrition* and what are its causes? (pp. 125-126)
43. Explain what the author means by *Apprehension* (p. 128)

44. There are many reasons why Moses should not have been apprehensive about fulfilling the mission he was assigned to by the one and only Jehovah. What are a few of these reasons? (pp. 131-132)
45. Give and discuss the threefold treatment the Lord gave to Peter to help him overcome his prejudice. (pp. 134-135)

Chapter Ten:

(46- 48) Name three of the missionaries from the past listed in this chapter that greatly inspired you. Discuss what stood out to you most from their lives and their ministry.

46.

47.

48.

Chapter Eleven:

(49- 50) Discuss two of the missionaries from the present listed in this chapter that greatly inspire you. Discuss what stands out to you most from their lives and their ministry.

49.

50.